BIBLICAL NUMEROLOGY

BIBLICAL NUMEROLOGY

by

John J. Davis

BAKER BOOK HOUSE
Grand Rapids, Michigan

Library of Congress Catalog Card Number: 68-19207

ISBN: 0-8010-2813-2

First printing, December 1968
Second printing, August 1971
Third printing, July 1973
Fourth printing, January 1975

PHOTOLITHOPRINTED BY CUSHING - MALLOY, INC.
ANN ARBOR, MICHIGAN, UNITED STATES OF AMERICA
1975

TO

ARTHUR AND MAY NICHOLS
whose prayers and
interest have been
a constant source
of encouragement in
the Christian ministry.

ACKNOWLEDGMENTS

The author desires to express gratitude to Dr. John C. Whitcomb, Dr. Jesse Humberd, Dr. S. Herbert Bess, and Dr. Homer A. Kent, Sr. for their constructive suggestions regarding the structure and content of this work.

Appreciation is also expressed to my wife who spent many hours in typing this manuscript. To Mr. Cornelius Zylstra, editor, Baker Book House, the author is indebted for many valuable suggestions concerning final preparations of this volume.

John J. Davis
Grace Theological Seminary
Winona Lake, Indiana

CONTENTS

LIST OF TABLES 11

1. INTRODUCTION 15

PART I. THE NATURE OF BIBLICAL NUMBERS

2. THE STRUCTURE AND SYNTAX OF
      BIBLICAL NUMBERS 25
    A. Old Testament 25
    B. New Testament 40

3. THE CONVENTIONAL USE OF NUMBERS . . 49
    A. The Functions of Conventional Numbers . . 49
    A. Problems Relative to Conventional Numbers . 55
    C. Summary 90

4. THE RHETORICAL USE OF NUMBERS 93
    A. The Climactic Use of Numbers 93
    B. The Idiomatic Use of Numbers 100
    C. Summary 102

5. THE SYMBOLIC USE OF NUMBERS 103
    A. The Origin of Symbolic Numbers 104
    B. The Development of Symbolic Numbers . . . 106
    C. The Interpretation of Symbolic Numbers . . 115
    D. Summary 124

6. THE MYSTICAL USE OF NUMBERS 125

    A. Historical Survey of the Concept of
       Mystical Numbers 125

    B. Supposed Values of Bible (Mystical) Numerics 134

    C. Methodology Employed in the Analysis of
       Mystical Numbers 136

7. SUMMARY AND CONCLUSIONS 153

    Conclusion 155

8. BIBLIOGRAPHY 157

LIST OF TABLES

Transliteration 14

1. Hebrew Numerals 28

2. Hebrew Alphabetic Numerals 39

3. Early Greek Acrophonic Numerals 42

4. Greek Alphabetic Numerals 43

5. The Two Numberings 76

6. & 7. The Interpretations of Symbolic Numbers . . . 122

INTRODUCTION

TRANSLITERATION

Whenever possible, Hebrew and Greek words have been transliterated according to the following form:

Greek	Consonants	Vocalization
α — a	א — '	— ā
ἀ — a	ב — b, ḇ	— a
ε — e	ג — g, g̱	— e
η — ē	ד — d, ḏ	— ē
ο — o	ה — h	— ê
ω — ō	ו — w	— i
ζ — z	ז — z	— î
	ח — ḥ	
θ — th	ט — ṭ	— o
ξ — x	י — y	— û
υ — u	כ — k, ḵ	— u
φ — ph	ל — l	— ( )e
χ — ch	מ — m	
Ψ — ps	נ — n	
' — h	ס — s	
	ע — '	
	פ — p, p̱	
	צ — ṣ	
	ק — q	
	ר — r	
	שׂ — ś	
	שׁ — š	
	ת — t, ṯ	

Chapter 1

INTRODUCTION

The writer's interest in the subject of Biblical numbers has extended over a number of years, but it has been the constant confrontation with numerical problems in the Bible and the realization that there was a serious lack of adequate materials on this subject that has stimulated acute interest in analyzing these problems systematically. After rather extensive correspondence and research in this subject area, it was apparent that the student of Biblical exegesis did not have adequate source materials with which to handle numerological problems in the sacred text. In fact, the last noteworthy effort to examine the numerical phenomena of the Scriptures in any depth was the work of Eduard König in Hasting's dictionary of the Bible published over sixty years ago.[1] An expanding corpus of research materials is readily available in almost every area of Biblical studies with the exception of numerological considerations. To what shall one attribute this apparent neglect? Perhaps writers have overlooked the subject intentionally because they felt it to be trivial and open to misrepresentation. There is no doubt that if one concentrates his efforts in this area, he might well be misunderstood and classified among the rather extensive list of speculative numerologists who have endeavored to unlock the many "deep mysteries" of holy writ, and in so doing have blurred the very image they intended to clarify. J. B. Segal has observed the following with regard to this problem:

> Statistics of the Bible, like the calculations of the Great Pyramid of Egypt, have a fatal attraction for cranks and crackpots — even for wise men in their less guarded moments.[2]

The observations of Segal are confirmed by the fact that the greater proportion of books on this general subject are produced

[1]"Number," *A Dictionary of the Bible,* ed. James Hastings (New York: Charles Scribner's Sons, 1900).

[2]"Numerals in the Old Testament," *Journal of Semitic Studies,* X (Spring, 1965), p. 2.

by men, who, at the expense of sound methodology, have sought to present spectacular and unusual ideas employing the numbers of the Bible.

Another reason for the apparent neglect of interest in this area is both the direct and indirect influence of negative criticism upon Biblical commentators. According to H. J. Cook, scholars are generally of the same opinion with regard to Biblical numbers and their consensus is:

> The numbers cannot be trusted, and difficulties presented by them can be solved by disregarding any of them.[3]

There is no doubt that the Bible does indeed present problems in its various uses of numbers, but it hardly seems justified that all numbers of the Bible should be regarded as untrustworthy because such problems exist. It is the view of Cyrus H. Gordon that all Biblical numerals down to the United Monarchy reflect schematic numbers taken over from epic traditions and therefore should not be taken seriously.[4] Scholars differ widely on which numbers are to be taken at face value and which should be regarded as schematic.

Upon careful examination of the literary productions of such critics, it will be observed that there are two underlying factors which produce the above conclusions. First, there is the *a priori* assumption that the Scriptures are prescientific and therefore cannot be accurate or trustworthy in matters of technical or scientific import. Such an assumption, however, must be regarded as fallacious, for there is a considerable body of literature (scientific and non-scientific) which is perfectly accurate and trustworthy in spite of its prescientific origins.[5] Where is the scholar who will assert that observations made in the "scientific era" must be valid and accurate because they were made in that era? Such a proposition would be rejected by all, for infallible scientific opinion has yet to be realized even in the "space age." The second underlying factor for critical opinion is

---

[3]"Pekah," *Vetus Testamentum,* XIV (April, 1964), p. 123.

[4]*Introduction to Old Testament Times* (Ventor: Ventor Publishers, Inc., 1953), p. 104, n.6.

[5]E.g., Mathematical observations of the Greeks, records of some early historians and church fathers, etc.

the fundamental teaching on their part that the Old Testament is a record of the development or evolution of the religion and culture of ancient Israel. According to many scholars, the early records of the Bible reflect traditions that have been seriously defaced by later scribes and redactors and therefore should be handled with considerable suspicion.

The Issues Involved

This study is focused on two pivotal problems related to Biblical numbers. First is the problem of the nature of Biblical numbers. There appears to be considerable debate as to the form of numbers as they appeared in the earlier manuscripts of the Bible. Careful consideration will be given to the orthography and paleography of numerals as they appear in both contemporary inscriptional material and the Bible.

The second principal problem with which this investigation is concerned is the proper interpretation of Biblical numbers. Since there is wide diversity of opinion as to the value of numbers, there will quite naturally follow a variety of methods of interpreting such numbers. It is therefore paramount that the value and accuracy of Biblical numbers be determined and then one is in a position to determine interpretive principles.

The Scope of the Subject

The subject of Biblical numerology touches, in one way or another, every area in Biblical studies. The subject is vitally connected with the over-all field of theology and more specifically with the prophetic doctrines of the Bible.[6] The study of Biblical numbers is, of course, inseparable from the study of Biblical chronology. The whole chronological scheme of a scholar will rest on his interpretation of the numerical data of the Bible. Finally, the numbers of the Bible play an important role in the general area of hermeneutics, for numbers, as it will be shown, are important not only in conveying mathematical data, but in formulating literary stylisms.

---

[6]Compare, for example, the important role numbers play in the books of Daniel, Ezekiel and Revelation.

Definition of Terms

Numerology. This word is derived from the Latin *numerus,* a number and *logy,* science or study.[7] This term is employed in the general sense of "the study of numbers." It is to be distinguished from the term numerics, which according to most dictionaries, may refer to either the general study of numbers or the specific investigation of the mysteries of numbers. Whenever the term numerics is used in this study, it will have reference only to the study of symbolical or mystical numbers. The study of Biblical numerology, is therefore, the investigation of the nature and purpose of the numbers found in the Bible.

Numeral. This term will generally be employed to designate the figure, letter or word expressing a number.

Number. This is an amount or quantity of units. In many cases it is employed to describe a character or symbol which expresses mathematical values. In general, the term numeral will be used to express the symbol of the quantity under question while the term number will have reference to the quantity itself.

Methods and Conclusions

In any critical investigation which attempts to handle scientific data, certain procedures must be followed if valid and applicable conclusions are to be reached. It is important that the reader be fully aware that the validity of any conclusion in this area of study will be affected by the method of analysis employed.

In the preparation of this book three steps were followed. First, there was a systematic analysis, coordination and correlation of important numerical data in order to establish a sound context for definition. After this procedure was completed, careful examination and analysis of the data was undertaken. Finally, through evaluation and experimentation valid and consistent principles for the interpretation of Biblical numbers were

---

[7]Noah Webster and Jean L. McKechnie, eds., *Webster's New Twentieth Century Dictionary of the English Language,* unabridged (New York: The World Publishing Co., 1963), p. 1228.

sought. The presentation of numerical data in this study will reflect this fundamental methodology.

The investigation of Biblical numbers was carried out with some limitations. Perhaps the most outstanding problem faced was the lack of original Hebrew inscriptions. With the exception of the Gezer Calendar, the Siloam Inscription, Dead Sea Scrolls and ostraca from several sites, there was little to work with in the area of extended inscriptions in archaic Hebrew. The question which naturally arises is, why the lack of ancient Hebrew inscriptions? One possible answer would be that there were early Hebrew inscriptions in Palestine but they were not allowed to survive. Perhaps they were destroyed by the numerous invasions and occupations by hostile armies. Although other lands have suffered similar invasions, inscriptional materials have survived, even though in fragmentary form. Another possible answer to this question is that perhaps most ancient Hebrew inscriptions were written on papyrus or other perishable materials which have not survived the weather in Palestine.[8] In any event, the investigator must work with limited source materials in this area.

Along with the absence of original inscriptional material with which to compare the Biblical record, there was also a notable lack of trustworthy references in the specific area of numerology. Most of what has been written on this subject appears in fragmentary form. It was this situation and the encouragement of several scholars, whose work touches these areas, that caused this writer to pursue the subject systematically.

Some Basic Assumptions

This study assumes that the Bible is all that it claims to be, namely, the divinely inspired word of God. It is the view of this writer that the Bible does not reflect the religious inquiry of the Israelites and their subsequent religious development but God's special revelation to His people.[9] If the Scriptures are

---

[8]Martin Noth, *The History of Israel* (New York: Harper and Row, Publishers, 1960), p. 41.

[9]This is not to say that religious inquiry is not evident in the history of Israel, but such an inquiry cannot account for the unique phenomena of Scripture.

the product of the creative breath of God (II Tim. 3:16), they
must be regarded as inerrant in the autographs. This is not to
say that textual errors are not to be found in our present
manuscripts but it does assert that in spite of some textual problems, the text as a whole is a trustworthy record of all the
events it describes.

This study also presupposes the fundamental accuracy of
numbers as they appear in the Biblical text. It will be shown
that the general dismissal of Biblical numbers as worthless is not
justified. In fact, recent studies have shown that there is a
rather astounding degree of accuracy in the transmission of
Biblical numbers. Some years ago Solo Baron made a rather
thorough study of population figures for the period of the kings.
In the process he had occasion to collect and organize all verses
dealing with census figures. He took into account only the
numbers concerning the population as such, the army, involun-
tary and voluntary labor, cities, families, etc. On occasion he included the figures on sacrifices or on the amount of taxes. Dates,
measurements, etc., were not included. With these limitations
he assembled not less than 340 verses containing numbers. He
then attempted to establish the existing variants in either Hebrew manuscripts or the Greek, Latin or Aramaic versions as
well as occasional references to Josephus. The results were, as
he put it, "astonishing."[10] Out of 340 verses 260 had no variants
whatsoever. Of the remaining 80 verses only 7 had variants in
Hebrew manuscripts, 1 in Aquila, 8 in Syriac, 5 in Aramaic
versions, 7 in Josephus, and 52 in the LXX.[11] He found that
the largest number of variants were in I Samuel and I Kings
and the smallest in Judges and Chronicles.[12] This study seems
to justify the presupposition that there is fundamental accuracy
in the Biblical transmission of numbers. Other proofs for this
assumption will be presented in Chapter 3.

Aims of This Work

The specific aims of this work are three in number: (1) To

---

[10]"The Authenticity of the Numbers in the Historical Books of the Old
Testament," *Journal of Biblical Literature*, XLIX (1930), p. 288.
  [11]*Ibid.*, pp. 288-289.
  [12]*Ibid.*, p. 290.

collect, analyze and classify data relevant to numbers and their use in the Bible, (2) to define the nature and use of numbers in Scripture, and (3) by experimentation and evaluation to establish valid and consistent principles for the interpretation of Biblical numbers.

PART I

THE NATURE OF BIBLICAL NUMBERS

Chapter 2

THE STRUCTURE AND SYNTAX OF BIBLICAL NUMBERS

A. Old Testament

Terms Relative to Numbering and Counting

There are several factors that must be considered in the analysis of numbers. One such factor is the terminology employed in the context in which numbers are used. Since the following terms appear rather frequently in connection with numbers, a brief survey of these terms will be of great value when the particular significance of a number is sought. The terms are as follows:

1. *Sāpar,* "to count" (II Sam. 24:10; Ps. 56:9; Lev. 25:8; etc.).[1] There are three basic uses of this term. They are as follows:

   a. To count things, to learn of their number (Gen. 15:5; 41:49; Lev. 15:13; Deut. 16:9; etc.).

   b. To number, i.e., take account of, carefully observe and consider, reckon (Job 14:16; 31:41; 38:37; Ps. 56:9).[2]

   c. To measure (Gen. 41:49).[3]

2. *Mispār,* "a number" (Judg. 7:6; Ps. 147:4; etc.).[4] This term also has the idea of "recounting" (Judg. 7:15)[5] and it is used to designate a "few" (Num. 9:20; Hos. 12:16; Gen. 34:30).[6]

3. *Mānāh,* "to count, number, reckon."[7] The two basic uses of this term are:

---

[1]Francis Brown, S. R. Driver and Charles Briggs, *A Hebrew and English Lexicon of the Old Testament* (Oxford: The Clarendon Press, Corrected Impression, 1952), p. 707.

[2]*Ibid.*

[3]Ludwig Koehler and Walter Baumgartner, eds., *Lexicon in Veteris Testamenti Libros* (Leiden: E. J. Brill, 1958), p. 665.

[4]Brown, Driver, Briggs, *op. cit.,* p. 708.

[5]*Ibid.*

[6]Koehler and Baumgartner, *op. cit.,* p. 543.

[7]Brown, Driver, Briggs, *op. cit.,* p. 584.

a. To count, number (Gen. 13:16; Num. 23:10; II Kings 12:11; Ps. 147:4; etc.).

b. To reckon, assign, appoint (Isa. 65:12; 53:12; Gen. 13:16; I Kings 3:8; etc.).[8]

4. *Minyān* (Aramaic *menā'*), "number" (Ezra 6:17).

5. *Pāqaḏ*, "to attend, visit, muster."[9]

A common usage of this form is to convey the idea of numbering for military organization (I Sam. 11:8; 13:15; Num. 1:3, 19, 44, 49; Exod. 30:12, 13, 14; etc.).[10] According to M. H. Pope this word has an even larger usage in the Old Testament. He states that the form conveys the following ideas:

> Attend to, visit, muster. It is used of mustering and reviewing troops, of taking census of population, and of accounting and inventory of goods, and is thus equivalent to a verb of counting; its passive participle is used to designate persons or things counted.[11]

The terms, when in juxtaposition with numerals, are an important aid in ascertaining the precise function of those numerals.

The Construction of Numbers

Israel, like Assyria,[12] Egypt, Greece and Rome, used the decimal system of counting. The numbers found in the Hebrew text of the Old Testament are always written out.

Cardinal Numbers. The numeral "one" (*'eḥāḏ* Fem. *'aḥat*) is considered an adjective on the basis of its form and use. It follows its noun and agrees with it in gender. The numeral "two" is a noun and both feminine (*šetayim*) and masculine (*šenayim*) forms are abstract in the dual.[13] The number "two"

---

[8]*Ibid.*

[9]*Ibid.*, p. 823.

[10]*Ibid.*

[11]"Numbers," *The Interpreter's Dictionary of the Bible*, George Arthur Buttrick, ed. (Nashville: Abingdon Press, 1962), p. 562.

[12]The Sexigesimal system of counting was also popularly used in Assyria.

[13]Gesenius, E. Kautzsh and A. E. Cowley, *Hebrew Grammar* (Oxford: The Clarendon Press, 1957), p. 288. Hereafter referred to as Gesenius, Kautzsh, Cowley.

is regarded by Semites generally as the extension of "one." This fact, according to J. B. Segal, is clear from the morphology of the dual number.[14] When the number "two" is used as a construct, it precedes the word numbered and, as an absolute, it stands after the word in apposition. The numerals 3 to 10 are feminine nouns, and when in construct, they precede the word numbered, but when used appositionally the absolute may either precede the word numbered or follow it.[15] They are peculiar in that:

> . . . the numerals connected with a masculine substantive take the feminine form, and those with a feminine substantive take the masculine form.[16]

The numerals from 11 to 19 are formed by placing the unit before the 10. The waw conjunctive is omitted and the two words are not joined into one (e.g., 'aḥaḏ 'āśār, "eleven"). The tens are denoted by the plural forms of the units (e.g., šāloš, "three"; šelošîm, "thirty"). The numeral 20 is an exception to this observation for it is the plural of ('eśer) 10. The units, when connected to the tens are so done by the use of the conjunction, thus (šiḇîm wešiḇ'ah–70 and 7=77).
The remaining numbers are substantives.[17]

Ordinal Numbers. The Ordinal numbers from 1 to 10 are adjectives which follow the noun and agree with it in gender. The Ordinal "first" is expressed by the form ri'šon, from ro'š, "head" or "beginning." The Ordinals from 2 to 10 are formed from the corresponding Cardinals by adding the ending ִ‍ֹ‍ , before which another ִ‍ also is generally inserted between the second and third radicals.[18] From 11 upwards the Cardinal numbers serve as Ordinals. The context will generally indicate the translation required. Fractions may be expressed by feminine forms of the Ordinals (e.g., šelišît – "a third").

---

[14]*Op. cit.*, p. 3.
[15]In Semitic grammar generally, the noun following the numerals 3 to 10 is in the plural, but from 11 onwards, the noun is in the singular. See J. B. Segal, *op. cit.*, p. 4.
[16]Gesenius, Kautzsh and Cowley, *op. cit.*, p. 287.
[17]See Table #1 p. 28 for a list of these and other numbers discussed here.
[18]Gesenius, Kautzsh, and Cowley, *op. cit.*, p. 292.

The Notation of Numbers

Systems of notation. In the Hebrew Old Testament, numbers are spelled out, but this was not always the case in other contemporary literature. There were three possibilities for the writing of numerals other than full words.

TABLE 1

HEBREW NUMERALS

Cardinal Numbers[19]		Ordinal Numbers[20]	
1.	'ehāḏ	First.	ri'šon
2.	šenayim	Second.	šēnî
3.	šelošāh	Third.	šelîšî
4.	'arbā'āh	Fourth.	rebî'î
5.	ḥemišāh	Fifth.	ḥemîšî
6.	šišāh	Sixth.	šišî
7.	šib'āh	Seventh.	šebî'î
8.	šemonāh	Eighth.	šemînî
9.	tiš'āh	Ninth.	teši'î
10.	'ešārāh	Tenth.	'esîrî
20.	'esrîm		
100.	(Fem.) mē'āh		
200.	(Dual) ma'tayim		
1000.	'eleḇ		

---

[19]Absolute forms when used with masculine nouns.
[20]Masculine forms.

First, acrophonic systems were used in which the initial letter of the word by which a number was called was used to represent the number itself (e.g., Γ = pente = 5). This system was mainly employed by the early Greeks.[21] The second system employed was the alphabetic system in which the sequential characters of the alphabet served as numbers. Finally, there was the "sign system" or as Jack Finegan calls, it the "arbitrary sign system."[22] This system used accepted or conventional symbols for numbers. Some inscriptional materials evidence knowledge of only one system while others contain several systems in one text.

The earliest numerals of which we have definite record were simply straight marks for the small numbers, with some special form for 10. These symbols appear in Egypt as early as the First Dynasty (c. 3400 B.C.), and in Mesopotamia as early as c. 3000 B.C. These dates long precede the first known inscriptions containing numerals in other lands such as in India (third cent. B.C.), China (third cent. B.C.) and Crete (c. 1200 B.C.). These symbols appeared as follows:

Egyptian Hieroglyphic (c. 3400 B.C.) .... I ∩
Egyptian Hieratic (c. 3400 B.C.) .... I Λ
Creten Inscriptions (c. 1200 B.C.) .... I —
Sumerian and Later Inscriptions .... ∨ ＜

The vertical marks, I, I I, I I I etc., may possibly be representations of the fingers as used in counting and computing, a linguistic trace of which is found in the word "digit."

Cuneiform Inscriptions

Sumerian and Babylonian. The numeral notations of the Sumerians was that of ideographical symbol. One was written ▷— (AS) or 𐏒 (DIS) as is the case in some of the Drehem tablets.[23] Two was written ⟝ (TAB) or 𐏒𐏒 (MIN), three

---

[21]Full discussion of this phenomenon will appear later. See p. 41 ff.

[22]*Handbook of Biblical Chronology* (Princeton: Princeton University Press, 1964), p. 3.

[23]William Nesbit, *Sumerian Records From Drehem* (New York: Columbia University Press, 1914), pp. 13, 14, 67.

ҮҮҮ (EŠ).[24] Nine was written ◁ Ү⤚ The sign ◁
= 10, Ү⤙ (LAL) ="subtract," and ◥ = –1). The whole
expression was ✕-lal-I or 10-1.[25] The numeral 10 was
represented by a corner wedge (◁). Twenty and other multiples of 10 were merely additional corner wedges (e.g., ◁◁◁◁
= 40).

What has been observed with reference to Sumerian numerals
also applies to the Akkadian or Babylonian system. The symbols
for the most part are exactly the same but having different
phonetic values. The symbol Ү served also for 60, 600 and in
general for 10×60^n; similarly, the symbol for 10 served
for 10×60^n, the context telling what particular value was indicated. The sign for 10 was sometimes written ◯ using the
circular end of the stylus instead of the pointed. In later
inscriptions numbers such as 19 would not be written 20
– 1 but ◁ ∇∇∇∇∇∇∇∇∇ = 10 + 3 + 3 + 3 = 19.[26]

Ugaritic. Numbers were written both ideographically and in
full words at Ugarit. In general it can be said that in adminis-
trative documents ideographic symbols were generally employed[27] whereas in literary documents full words were employed. Gordon observes:

> We know as much as we do about the numerals in Ugaritic
> because the scribes do not as a rule represent the numeral
> ideographically in the literary texts.[28]

---

[24]*Ibid.,* compare also Samuel Kramer, *The Sumerians* (Chicago: The
University of Chicago Press, 1963), p. 91f.

[25]Cf. William Nesbit, *op. cit.,* tablet VI, R, 3, p. 28.

[26]Further discussion of these systems may be found in the following
volumes:

G. A. Cooke, *A Text-Book of North Semitic Inscriptions* (Oxford: The
Clarendon Press, 1903).

I. J. Gelb, *Morphology of Akkadian* (Chicago: by the author, 1952).

"Number," *Encyclopedia Britannica* (Chicago: William Benton, Publisher,
1960), Vol. XVI.

[27]Cyrus H. Gordon, *Ugaritic Handbook,* II (Rome: Pontifical Bible
Institute, 1948), documents 81, 82, 108, 113, 115, 300, 301, etc.

[28]*Ibid.* I, p. 32.

In Ugaritic the same symbols are used for numerals as in Sumerian and Akkadian (𐎟 = 1 and 𐎟 = 10, etc.). The proximity of the people of Ras Shamra (Ugarit) to Palestine makes their numerological notations of great significance to the Bible student. There will be occasion to refer back to their notation patterns.[29]

The Phoenicians also, like the Babylonians, used signs for numerical. notation. Their inscriptions, however, display frequent use of both symbol and written words. In some inscriptions both were used in the same text. In the Eshmunazar inscription this is illustrated when the following appears: ‏ו, ‎III‎⁓‏עהיבעברא‏ ‏עבש‏.[30] According to König there are some inscriptions which have written numbers only. He sees in this a parallel to the Siloam inscription which exhibits the same phenomenon.[31]

Other Inscriptions and Numerical Systems

Egyptian. Egyptian Hieroglyphic texts indicate numerals much the same way as cuneiform texts. "One" is indicated by a vertical line, and the numbers from "two" to "nine" by vertical strokes placed side by side. Ten is denoted by ∩ , twenty ∩∩ , thirty ∩∩∩ , seventy ∩∩∩ ∩∩∩∩ , etc. The sign for 100 is ℮ and 200 is formed by doubling that sign ℮℮ .[32] The Ordinals were formed by adding ଃ -nu to the numeral, with the exception of the "first" which was written 𓂋𓏏 . Second would be ∥ଃ, third ∥∥ ଃ, fourth ∥∥∥ଃ, etc.[33] How much the ancient Hebrew knew of this system can only be conjectured. Moses and Joseph undoubtedly had a rather thorough knowledge of it.

Aramaic. The Aramaic numbers found in the Bible are, like the Hebrew numbers, written out in word form. Grammatically,

---

[29] *Infra,* p. 95.

[30] Eduard König, *op. cit.,* p. 561.

[31] *Ibid.*

[32] E. A. Wallis Budge, *First Steps in Egyptian* (London: Kegan Paul, Trench, Trubner & Co., 1895), p. 32.

[33] E. A. Wallis Budge, *Easy Lessons in Egyptian Hieroglyphics* (London: Kegan Paul, Trench, Trubner, & Co., 1899), p. 129.

they function much in the same manner.[34] In extra-biblical inscriptions, however, two systems are employed. For example, in a letter written in the early fifth century B.C. from 'Arsam to 'Artahont reference is made to thirteen slaves in Egypt. The notation appears as follows: ‏כל גברן‎\\\ ("All 13 men").[35] In an agreement dated 495 B.C. the dateline is recorded in the following manner:

‏שנת אפף רח (י) ל‎   ‏בי (ז) ם \\‎

‏לדריוש מלכא‎

> "On the 2nd day of the month Epiphi of
> the 27th year of king Darius. . ."[36]

Note that "2nd" was represented by the sign ‖.

The 27th year was written ‏שנת‎ ‖‖ ‖‖ | ‏‎   (‏ר‎ = 20
+ ‖‖ ‖‖ | = 7). In a "grant of Building Rights" dated 471 B.C. the same notation patterns occur:

‏יום‎ ‏הו לאלול‎ ‏ב‎ ‖ ‖‖ ‖‖

‏לפחנס שנת‎ ‏חשיארש‎ ‏מלכא...‎

> "On the 18th of Elul, that is the 28th
> day of Pahons, year 15 of king Xerxes. . ."[37]

This system of notation was not only used in datelines but it is found frequently in the body of the text.[38] In other documents of the same character both systems of notation were employed. In a "Contract for a Loan" (456 B.C.) the number "four" is written | ‖‖ and ‏ארבעה‎ .[39]

The question that naturally arises at this point is, did the Biblical writers have knowledge of these systems and if so, did

---

[34]Franz Rosenthal, *A Grammer of Biblical Aramaic* (Wiesbaden: Otto Harrassowitz, 1961), p. 31f.

[35]G. R. Driver, *Aramaic Documents of the 5th Century B.C.* (Oxford: The Clarendon Press, 1957), pp. 26, 27.

[36]A. Cowley, ed., *Aramaic Papyri of the Fifth Century B.C.* (Oxford: The Clarendon Press, 1923), Text No. 1, p. 1.

[37]*Ibid.*, Text No. 5, pp. 10-11. (Italics mine).

[38]*Ibid.*, lines 4, 7, and Text No. 8, pp. 21-25, lines 5, 14, 21.

[39]*Ibid.*, Text No. 10, pp. 24-32, lines 3, 4. See also Eduard König, *op. cit.*, p. 561, for a discussion of the Old Aramaic inscriptions of Zinjirli.

they use them? As previously noted, the Aramaic numerals of the Old Testament are written out in full.[40] Since Aramaic documents (fifth to fourth centuries B.C.), Nabatean and Palmyrene inscriptions used special signs for numerals, Allrik concludes:

> As for the Hebrews themselves, there is no doubt they too employed the same principles of numeral notation. Hebrew ostraca from the kingdoms regularly show vertical strokes for units.[41]

The lists of Nehemiah 7 and Ezra 2 in the Masoretic text show a number of differences even though they seem to refer to the same occasion and the same facts.[42] Numerous solutions to the problem have been offered. Some have supposed that the lists are from different occasions and the changes represent growth in the community. Another suggestion is that some numbers represent revisions based on additional information. Other scholars have related the discrepancies to the fact that confusion resulted because letters of the alphabet were used to designate numbers.[43] Allrik feels that some differences may be traced to the transmission of the present form of the text where numbers are spelled out in words. But on the whole, he concludes that the problem is solved by understanding the numbers to have originally been written with signs which in some cases were misunderstood. Others seem to be of the same opinion on this matter.

> The fact that we have no evidence for the early use of symbols for numbers among the Hebrews does not necessarily mean that they did not have and use some system of figures. At Ugarit the numerals in the literary texts are always spelled out, but in the administrative documents they are written ideographi

---

[40]*Supra,* p. 31.

[41]H. L. Allrik, "The Lists of Zerubbabel (Nehemiah 7 and Ezra 2) and the Hebrew Numeral Notation," *Bulletin of the American Schools of Oriental Research,* Number 136 (Dec. 1954), p. 24.

[42]*Ibid.,* p. 22. The numbers of Nehemiah's list are generally larger. This might indicate that they were, in some cases, estimates which were later revised.

[43]*Ibid.,* p. 21.

cally with Sumero-Akkadian symbols. The old Aramaic inscriptions from Zenjirli, the Aramaic documents from Elephantine,
and some Phoenician inscriptions spell out the numerals and
also use figures. In the Eshmunazar Inscription the date is
given in both words and in figures. On the Aramaic lion
weights from Nineveh [8th-7th centuries BC.] the numbers
are doubly represented in words and figures. In South Arabic inscriptions also, the numbers are sometimes written in
full and sometimes represented by figures.

It seems likely that Israel would also have used symbols
since their neighbors did.[44]

According to G. A. Reisner and others, ostraca from Samaria
show more than twenty occurrences of what has been judged
to be 15 consisting of a sign for 10 looking like a Greek
Lambda, and a sign for 5 like an early *gimel* having an upright
line with a horizontal top-stroke to the left.[45] Similar signs were
used in the Tell ed-Duweir letters before the fall of Judah to
the Babylonians.[46] This data appears to negate the value of
William Taylor Smith's assertion in the *International Bible Encyclopedia:*

> No special signs for the expression of Numbers in writing
> can be proved to have been in use among the Hebrews before
> the exile.[47]

If Smith's reference relates to proof from Biblical data alone,
his argument is somewhat justified, but it appears that even

---

[44]M. H. Pope "Number," *Op. cit.,* p. 563.

[45]*Harvard University Excavations of Samaria 1908-1910* (Harvard University Press, 1924), Vol. I, pp. 224-248. Recent discoveries at Tell Arad
seem to warrant a reconsideration of these conclusions, however. It is the
view of Yohanan Aharoni that these special signs for numbers are really
hieratic numerals. Cf. Yohanan Aharoni, "The Use of Hieratic Numerals
in Hebrews Ostraca and the Shekel Weights," *Bulletin of the American
Schools of Oriental Research,* Number 184 (December, 1966). This re-
evaluation of the numerical signs not only carries with it mathematical
significance, but important cultural implications as well (cf. *ibid.,* p. 19).

[46]W. F. Albright, "The Lachish Letters After Five Years" *Bulletin of
the American Schools of Oriental Research,* Number 82 (April 1941).

[47]"Number," *The International Standard Bible Encyclopedia,* James Orr
ed. (Chicago: The Howard-Severance Co., 1925) IV, p. 2157.

though the existing manuscripts of the Old Testament do not evidence knowledge of such notation, the scribes of Israel surely must have made use of such a system. The Hebrews employed literary idioms that were used among the inhabitants of Canaan and for important building projects they used contemporary structural patterns ("header-stretcher" wall construction and casemate defensive walls) and Phoenician labor.[48] It seems reasonable to conclude that such a common literary phenomenon would also have been employed. To what extent Biblical writers employed such a system can only be conjectured. Merrill Unger argues for this view but assumes that it was the alphabetic method of writing numerals that caused some of the existing textual problems.

> But, though, on the one hand it is certain that in all existing manuscripts of the Hebrew text of the Old Testament the numerical expressions are written at length, yet, on the other, the variations in the several versions between themselves and from the Hebrew text, added to the evident inconsistencies in numerical statements between certain passages of that text itself, seem to prove that some shorter mode of writing was originally in vogue, liable to be misunderstood by copyists and translators. These variations appear to have proceeded from the alphabetic method of writing numbers.[49]

There is some doubt as to the antiquity of the alphabetic method of numerical notation and therefore this solution is rather tenuous.[50] But it appears that all peoples in the fertile crescent area employed at least two notation systems, the symbols and the fully written words.[51]

Minoan Linear A. and Linear B. Because of the arduous investigations of Michael Ventris, John Chadwick[52] and Cyrus

---

[48]Cf. I Kings 5.

[49]*Unger's Bible Dictionary* (Chicago: Moody Press, 1957), p. 799.

[50]*Infra.*, pp. 38, 39.

[51]John D. Davis, *A Dictionary of the Bible* (Grand Rapids: Baker Book House, 1954), p. 546.

[52]See Michael Ventris and John Chadwick, *Documents in Mycenaean Greek* (Cambridge: The University Press, 1956).

Gordon, scholars now have a good knowledge of the nature of early Cretan inscriptional materials. The Minoan inscriptions according to Cyrus Gordon, constitute an important bridge between the Northwest Semitic world and the Aegean world.[53] Their findings seem to indicate that there was not only linguistic affinity between the two literary worlds, but also arithmetical similarities. The numerals for Linear A are as follows: | one, − ten, O one hundred, ⊕ one thousand, ⊕ ten thousand. The arithmetical methods of Linear A and B have been analyzed by W. French Anderson with satisfying and interesting results. Addition, for example, involved only the process of counting. If OOO = ||| (323) was to be added to OO = = | (241), it was only necessary to count how many times each of the separate symbols is used in the two numbers, and the accumulated sum is the answer. In the problem cited, there was a total of five hundreds (OOOOO), six tens (≡ ≡), and four units (||||). The sum, therefore, of the above number is OOO ≡ ≡ !! (564). Symbols like the above were also used in subtraction, multiplication and division.[54]

Hebrew. Hebrew inscriptions show a variety of systems of notation. It has been this factor which has caused the rather heated debate concerning the original notation system(s) employed by the Biblical writers. In Hebrew inscriptions from *c.* 1000 B.C. to *c.* 400 B.C. at least two methods of numerical notation are evident. The most common, and the one that appears in the earlier inscriptions is that of writing the number out in full. The Siloam inscription which was discovered in 1880 in the rock wall of the lower entrance to the tunnel of Hezekiah south of the temple area in Jerusalem, employs such notation patterns. The first half of this inscription is apparently missing, but that which remains is in clear archaic Hebrew. Its contents and script point to the reign of Hezekiah, about 715-

[53]*Ugaritic Handbook II* (Rome: Pontifical Bible Institute, 1947), p. 204; "The Minoan Bridge: Newest Frontier in Biblical Studies," *Christianity Today* (March 15, 1963), p. 3 ff.

[54]"Arithmetical Procedure in Minoan Linear A and in Minoan-Greek Linear B" *American Journal of Archaeology*, Vol. 62, No. 3 (July 1958), p. 563.

687.[55] Lines 5 and 6 of the text transliterated into square Hebrew appears as follows:

המים מן המוצא אל הברכה במאתים

ואלף אמה ומ [א] ת אמה היה גבה הצר

על ראש החצבם

"The waters from the spring to the pool,
1200 cubits. And 100 cubits was the height
of the rock above the head of the quarry-
men."

It will be seen that both numbers are represented in full writing. Other archaic Hebrew inscriptions such as the Lachish Letters, Gezer Calendar, and fragmentary inscriptions on seals and ostraca, either do not furnish us with information as to the numerical notation patterns or such notations are limited and not clear.[56]

Moabite. Perhaps the most significant literary production extant today of Moabite origin is the Mesha or Moabite Stone. This inscription was discovered intact in 1868 but was later broken into pieces by the Arabs. Today it is in the Louvre in Paris. The date of the stone is variously placed between 849 B.C. and 820 B.C. This inscription is of significance for our study because it contains six numerical expressions all of which are written out in full. They occur in lines 2, 8, 16, 20, 28, 29.[57]

The method of using symbols for numbers (such as |, ||, |||, etc.) does not seem to have been widely used among the Hebrews in the earlier periods. This conclusion is, of course, based on a minimal amount of epigraphical evidence. Since the Phoenicians and the people at Ugarit used such symbols

---

[55]This conclusion seems to be reaffirmed by II Kings 20:20 and II Chron. 32:30.

[56]Lachish Ostraca No. XIX which is a list of names and figures is discussed by H. L. Ginsberg, "Lachish Ostraca New and Old" *Bulletin of the American Schools of Oriental Research,* No. 80 (Dec. 1940), p. 12. The inscription is not clear enough to draw any substantial conclusions with regard to its numerical notations. See previous discussion on this matter on p. 34.

[57]W. H. Bennett, *The Moabite Stone* (Edinburgh: T. & T. Clark, 1911), pp. 62-63.

there is no reason for denying such usage to the ancient Hebrews. It is interesting to note that in the Dead Sea Scrolls
numbers are written out just as they are in the Masoretic text.

The third method that was employed for writing numerals
was the alphabetic method. In this system the units are denoted by *alep - tet*, the tens by *yod - ṣade*, the first 400 by
qop - taw, 500 - 900 by *taw* plus the symbol for the other hundreds. The thousands are indicated by the units with two dots
above ($\ddot{\aleph} = 1000$). For the numbers 15 and 16 the combinations of $9 + 6$ and $9 + 7$ were used to avoid the short forms of
the divine name *yh* and *yw*. The antiquity of this practice is
quite uncertain. This system appears never to have been used
in the Old Testament. Its earliest use to date among the Hebrews seems to be on Jewish coins which have been dated in
the reign of Maccabean Simon (143-135 B.C.). It should not be
supposed, however, that this was the only method employed,
for even here numbers were spelled out. The Mishna (Shek.
III:2) states that the three chests used in the second temple
were marked *alep, bet, gimel*, which might indicate knowledge
of the system, but the actual value or meaning of *alep, bet,
gimel*, is obscure. König seems to feel that the system had some
early use but that a sign system was probably earlier.

> . . . this alphabetic method of indicating numbers need not
> have been the only one employed by the Hebrews in the course
> of centuries. They may have in earlier days employed one of
> the lineo-acrostic systems which were in use among their eastern
> or western neighbors, and may have passed from this to the
> alphabetic method, just as the Greeks and Syrians did. It is,
> indeed, almost more probable that the Hebrews copied than
> that they avoided the practice of their neighbors.[58]

Driver also argues for the view that the Hebrew did use a
notation system other than full words but denies that the alphabetic system was used in ancient times.

> There is no ground for supposing . . . that in ancient times
> numerals were represented in Hebrew MSS by the letters of
> the alphabet. If the numerals were not written in full, but
> expressed by symbols, the ancient Hebrews, it is reasonable to

---

[58]*Op. cit.*, p. 562.

suppose, would have adopted a system similar to that in use amongst their neighbors, found equally in Phoenician, Palmyrene, Nabataean, and Old Aramaic inscriptions, and used also in Syriac.[59]

The skepticism of these scholars with regard to the antiquity of this system among the Hebrews seems justified in the light of present data. Not only is there a lack of evidence for the use of the alphabetic system during the Old Testament era, but it does not appear in other inscriptions until the Hellenistic period. R. A. H. Gunner observes that:

> The idea of using the letters of the alphabet for numerals originated from Greek influence, and, as far as is known, first appeared on Maccabean coins.[60]

TABLE 2

HEBREW ALPHABETIC NUMERALS

Alep = 1	Lamed = 30
Bet = 2	Mem = 40
Gimel = 3	Nun = 50
Dalet = 4	Samek = 60
He = 5	'Ayin = 70
Waw = 6	Pe = 80
Zayin = 7	Ṣade = 90
Ḥet = 8	Qop = 100
Ṭet = 9	Reš = 200
Yod = 10	S(h)in = 300
Kap = 20	Taw = 400

---

[59]*Notes on the Hebrew Text and the Topography of the Books of Samuel* (Oxford: The Clarendon Press, 1913), p. 97.

[60]"Number," *The New Bible Dictionary*, J. D. Douglas, ed. (Grand Rapids: Wm. B. Eerdmans Publishing Co., 1963), p. 895.

According to one scholar, the system should be traced beyond the Greeks to the Phoenicians.[61] This view, however, is without sufficient warrant. From what can be deduced from existing evidence, it appears that the Greeks were the originators of this system and from them it was copied by the inhabitants of Palestine and Egypt. The details concerning the origins of this system among the Greeks and their use of it will be discussed in a later section.[62]

B. New Testament

Terms Relative to Numbering and Counting

Numerical or arithmetical expressions in the Greek text of the New Testament are generally introduced by one of three expressions. In some cases these expressions are an aid to arriving at the interpretation of the number. They are as follows:

1. *Arithmeō*, "to number" (Matt. 10:30; Luke 12:7; Rev. 7:9).[63]

2. *Arithmos*, "a number." This term has a threefold usage. It is used to designate:

a. A fixed and definite number (John 6:10; Luke 22:3).

b. A number whose letters indicate a certain man (Rev. 13:18).

c. An indefinite number (Acts 6:7; 11:21; Rev. 20:8).[64]

3. *Psēphizō*, "to count with pebbles, to compute, calculate, reckon" (Luke 14:38; Rev. 13:18).[65]

Construction of Numbers

Cardinal numbers. The cardinal numbers, *heis* "one," *duo* "two," *treis* "three," *tessares* "four," are declinable in Greek (e.g.,

[61]See Eduard König, *op. cit.*, p. 561.
[62]Infra. pp. 42 ff, 140.
[63]Joseph H. Thayer, *A Greek-English Lexicon of the New Testament* (Edinburgh: T. & T. Clark, 1956), p. 73.
[64]*Ibid.*
[65]*Ibid.*, p. 676.

the Nom. of "one" is *heis* Masc., *mia* Fem., *hen* Neut.). The rest of the numbers are indeclinable up to two hundred, which, with the other hundreds, follows the plural of the first form of adjectives in *-oi, -ai, -a*.[66]

Ordinal numbers. The word for "first" in Greek is the superlative form *prōtos.* The remaining ordinals are derived from the stem of their cardinal numbers, and are declined like adjective of the first form.[67] In the reckoning of the days of the week, cardinals are sometimes used instead of ordinals.

When compound numbers are used, the largest is placed first and the smaller follow in order, with or without the conjunction *kai.*[68] It is interesting to note that no ordinals beyond "fifteenth" occur in the New Testament.[69]

Systems of Notation

There were, in ancient Greek, three methods of designating numerical values. The first system, and probably one of the earliest, was the acrophonic or that in which all the numeral signs are regularly the initial letters of the Greek words. For example, Γ (i.e., *pente*) = 5, Δ (i.e., *deka*) = 10, H (i.e., *hekaton*) = 100. The one exception to this observation is the unit 1 which was represented by a simple upright stroke. The "5" sign was utilized in a rather unique manner to designate larger quantities. If one wished to write 50 he would use the 5 sign Γ , and the 10 sign Δ, and combine them in the following manner: Δ . The combination of 5 and 100 was used for 500 (Γ) and Γ represented 5000.[70]

The earliest example of this system of notation is found in Attica and belongs to the fifth century, although there seems to be some evidence for dating the earliest uses back to the

---

[66]Samuel G. Green, *Handbook to the Grammar of the Greek Testament* (New York: Fleming H. Revell Co., 1912), p. 44.

[67]*Ibid.*, p. 45.

[68]Full discussion of the syntax of numbers is found in Green, *op. cit.*, p. 275ff. Cf. also James H. Moulton, *A Grammar of New Testament Greek* (Edinburgh: T. & T. Clark, 1957), I, p. 95f. and II, p. 167f.

[69]James Moulton, *Ibid.*, II, p. 173.

[70]A. G. Woodhead, *The Study of Greek Inscriptions* (Cambridge: The University Press, 1959), p. 108.

seventh century.[71] The acrophonic system was used extensively from these early centuries until about 300 B.C. when the alphabetic system, which was less cumbersome, came into popular use. This system remained in use in some areas until the first century B.C.[72]

The other system which was employed by the Greeks for numerical notations was the alphabetic. In this system values were assigned to the letters of the alphabet (e.g., *alpha* = 1, *beta* = 2, *epsilon* = 5, *rho* = 100).[73] In order to avoid difficulties in distinguishing numerals from normal letters in this system, either blank spaces were left on each side of the number or some special mark of punctuation was employed. Sometimes this mark would be a horizontal line just above the numeral. Woodhead points out that such marks tended to take several forms:

> The punctuation mark may be no more than a simple dot or pair of dots, but it may, especially in Hellenistic and Roman times, take a more fancy form, such as an ivy leaf.[74]

TABLE 3

EARLY GREEK ACROPHONIC NUMERALS[75]

I = 1	△△ = 20	HH = 200
II = 2	△△Γ = 25	⊢ = 500
III = 3	△△△ = 30	⊢HH = 700
IIII = 4	⊢ = 50	⊢HHΓI = 706
Γ = 5	⊢ Γ = 55	X = 1000
ΓI = 6	⊢ △ = 60	XX = 2000

---

[71]*Ibid.*
[72]*Ibid.*, p. 109. See Table No. 3, above.
[73]See Table No. 4, p. 43.
[74]*Ibid.*, p. 111.
[75]After Woodhead, *op. cit.*, p. 109.

Րıı = 7   🄰△△ı = 71   🄰 = 5000

△ = 10   H = 100   M = 10,000

△ıı = 12   H△ı = 111   MM = 20,000

△Ր = 15   HΡᴬ = 150

△Րı = 16

MM 🄰 ✕✕ Րᴴ HΡᴬ △△Ր ııı = 27,678

TABLE 4

GREEK ALPHABETIC NUMERALS

Alpha = 1   Xi = 60

Beta = 2   Omicron = 70

Gamma = 3   Pi = 80

Delta = 4   Koppa = 90

Epsilon = 5   Rho = 100

Vau = 6   Sigma = 200

Zeta = 7   Tau = 300

Eta = 8   Upsilon = 400

Theta = 9   Phi = 500

Iota = 10   Chi = 600

Kappa = 20   Psi = 700

Lambda = 30   Omega = 800

Mu = 40   Sampi = 900

Nu = 50

The real problem connected with this system is not how it was used in antiquity, but when it orginated and who was responsible for its inception.[76] It appears that the Greeks first used the letters of the alphabet as abbreviated labels, perhaps without numerical values in mind. Inscriptional materials from the fifth and fourth centuries B.C. seem to support this conclusion. Sterling Dow, who examined this problem rather thoroughly, writes the following:

> It is true, however, that the Athenians in numbering the ten subdivisions of each tribal group of dikastai, used the ten regular letters from *alpha* through *kappa* inclusive, omitting *stigma*. These were, in a sense, labels merely; the numerical value was of little or no account. Still it does seem likely that if the alphabetic system of numerals had been in common use in the late fifth or early fourth century B.C., or whenever the dikastai were first divided in 100 equal sections, then the sixth group would have had the symbol *stigma*, the seventh *zeta*, and so on. If the alphabetic system had been firmly implanted in the people's minds, *zeta* would have meant "seven" and to use it for the sixth group, as they actually did, would have seemed erroneous.[77]

It appears, from the evidence at hand, that the idea of alphabetic numbering was probably a fifth or fourth century B.C. development.[78] Its official use probably started in the third century B.C., although some would attribute its official use to the second century B.C.[79] The use of this system continued into the Byzantine period.[80]

The question which should be considered at this point is, What relation is there between this system and the alphabetic system employed by the Jews in the Hebrew script? As pre-

---

[76]The problem of its possible use by New Testament writers will be discussed later, *Infra.*, p. 144.

[77]Greek Numerals," *American Journal of Archaeology*, LVI (January, 1952), p. 22.

[78]The concepts and processes of this system may be the result of the direct or indirect influence of Pythagorus of the sixth century B.C.

[79]A. G. Woodhead, *op. cit.*, p. 111.

[80]Jack Finegan, *op. cit.*, p. 4.

viously noted there is no epigraphical evidence of the use of the Hebrew alphabet for numerals before the second century B.C.[81] It is the view of this writer that the Jews of the fourth-third centuries B.C. borrowed this idea from the Greeks under whose influence they came with the conquests of Alexander. There are a number of arguments which seem to support this proposition. First, there is no evidence that the alphabetic system was in use among the Jews prior to the Hellenization of Palestine. This is an argument from silence to be sure, but in the light of present evidence, it seems to be justified. Secondly, there is no evidence of the progressive development of such a system in early Hebrew inscriptional materials, whereas such is the case with Greek. The letters seem to have been employed first as labels for purposes of identification and summation[82] and then they appear with numerical values. In Hebrew, they appear as a fully-developed system at the outset, and they function in the same manner as the Greek system. Thirdly, this system did not have wide usage even after it was adopted by the Jews. It was used on coins of the Maccabean era but other inscriptions from that period indicate a preference, for fully-written words. Fourthly, if such a system did exist in early times, why did not Biblical scribes use it?[83] All numbers in the Old Testament are written out in full. As previously noted, all numbers that appear in the Biblical materials from Qumran are written out. Some of these MSS date back to 175 B.C. and were, no doubt, copied from very ancient Manuscripts. It is not likely that the Qumran scribes would have taken the liberty to convert numbers in the alphabetic system to fully-written words.

It can be seen, therefore, that the writers of Scripture had a number of systems which they could have employed. It appears, however, that they chose to write all numbers out with the possible exception of some of the census lists which may have originally employed special signs such as were used at Ugarit, and among the Aramaeans.

---

[81]*Supra,* pp. 28, 31.

[82]*Supra,* p. 34ff.

[83]The alleged use of Gematria in Gen 14:14 will be considered in a later chapter.

PART II

THE USES OF BIBLICAL NUMBERS

Chapter 3

THE CONVENTIONAL USE OF NUMBERS

The conventional use of a number is that use which is concerned primarily with the mathematical value of the number. Numbers used in this manner are designed to denote either a specific or a general mathematical quantity.

A. The Functions of Conventional Numbers

Mathematical processes. The ancient Hebrews were familiar with the four basic arithmetical operations, and they had at least an elementary control of fractions. They were not known for their aggressiveness in the area of technology and this is easily understood in the light of Mosaic legislation (Exod. 20: 4). Mathematics, architecture and art were, in the ancient Near East, inseparably linked with the religions of the various lands. Art and architecture were constant reflections of the religious ideas and ideals of both people and priests. Temples and monuments were not only characterized by inscriptions to the gods but by actual representations of those gods. In the light of these cultural patterns, it is easily understood why the Israelites were hesitant to engage in projects which could lead to violation of the law (cf. Deut. 4:15 ff.). When they did desire to build royal houses, skilled craftsman were brought in from Phoenicia.[1] In the light of this situation, we should not expect to discover large quantities of mathematical data in the Bible. In fact, it is quite difficult to ascertain the extent of mathematical developments in ancient Israel since arithmetical data are limited.

> Hardly any references to mathematical and astronomical subjects are found in the Bible, not even in a way which would indirectly enable us to arrive at some conclusion about the knowledge of the Jews after their return from the Babylonian exile. The nearest motive for such material would be the

---

[1] It might also be, however, that Phoenicians were used because of political pressure brought about by royal marriages (cf. I Kings 11:1-8).

building of the Tabernacle in Exodus and of the Solomonic
Temple (first book of Kings); yet the reference in the latter
(7:23) which has been often quoted as determining the number pi as 3, can be taken in many different aspects, and is
neither negatively nor positively conclusive.[2]

While the Bible does not contain large quantities of mathematical data, that which it does contain is accurate and trustworthy. The Bible is not a text book of either science or
mathematics but when it does treat such subjects, it does so
with complete dependability. Furthermore, in the light of ancient history, one should not expect the appearance of mathematical reasoning in the early chapters of the Bible, for such
reasoning, as is now understood by pure mathematicians, is the
contribution of the Greek-speaking communities of the Mediter-
ranean about 600 B.C.[3]

Only the simplest rules of arithmetic can be illustrated from
the Old Testament. Addition is used in Genesis 5:3-31 and in
Numbers 1:20-46. Subtraction is used, it may be assumed, by
Abraham in Genesis 18:28 ff. Knowledge of the process of multi-
plication is evident in Leviticus 25:8 and Numbers 3:46 ff. Division is used in Numbers 31:27 ff. According to Moulton "arithmetical processes are not represented in the New Testament."[4]

Fractions occur quite frequently in the Bible and when they
are employed, they are used properly. Many contemporary documents contain fractions but they were not used with serious
regard for accuracy. In the Ugaritic epic of Keret there is a
striking illustration of disregard for exactness in dealing with
fractions of diverse denominators. A series of catastrophes wiped
out Keret's progeny in its entirety, but piecemeal in the propor-
tions of 1/3, 1/4, 1/5, 1/6, and 1/7.[5] The sum of these fractions

---

[2]Abraham A. Fraenkel, "Jewish Mathematics and Astronomy," *Scripta
Mathematica*, XXV (1960), p. 47.

[3]Lancelot Hogben, *Mathematics in the Making* (Garden City: Doubleday and Co., 1960), p. 50.

[4]*Op. cit.*, II, p. 173. Moulton evidently adopts the A.S.V. reading
of Matt. 18:22. The expression is apparently ambiguous and its translation
is disputed.

[5]Cyrus H. Gordon, *Ugaritic Literature* (Roma: Pontificum Institutum
Biblicum, 1949), p. 67.

amounts to 459/420 = 153/140 = 1 13/14! Whether the ancient poet was aware of this error or not is not revealed. It is noteworthy that no such fractional errors exist in the Bible.

The Old Testament use of complementary fractions shows some influence of Egypt and Mesopotamia. The Hebrew idiom *pî šenayim* (litt. "two mouths") originally meant "two parts of three," or 2/3, exactly as the Akkadian *šenē pū* or *šenē pātu*, with which it is cognate.[6] Some of the fractions found in the Bible are as follows: 1/2, Exod. 25:10, 17; 1/3, II Sam. 18:2; 1/4, I Sam. 9:8; 1/5, Gen. 47:24; 1/6, Ezek. 46:14; 1/10, Exod. 16:36; 2/10, Lev. 23:13; 3/10, Lev. 14:10; 1/100, Neh. 5:11.

The mathematical concept of infinity may have been known in Biblical times for in Revelation 7:9 there is reference to the redeemed which are "a great multitude, which no man could number." In concrete imagery the Old Testament expresses the same idea, e.g., Genesis 13:16 reads "I will make your descendants as the dust of the earth: so that if one can count the dust of the earth, your descendants also can be counted" (RSV).[7]

Specific quantities. Perhaps the most common use of numbers in the Bible is the denotation of a specific quanitity. In most cases this usage is very easy to identify, but there are some places in the Bible where it is difficult to know whether a number represents a specific quantity or just a rounded number or approximation.[8] Normally, when a definite quantity is under consideration, the hundreds and/or units will be included in the number. Extended discussion of this usage is not necessary, for the interpretation of such numbers is obvious.

Rounded numbers. The use of a definite numerical expression in an indefinite sense is the fundamental idea behind round numbers. In many cases the writers of Scripture felt it unnecessary to provide the reader with exact detailed enumerations or

---

[6]Cf. Theophilus G. Pinches, *An Outline of Assyrian Grammar* (London: Henry J. Glaisher, 1910), p. 18.

Theo Bauer, *Akkadische Lesestücke*, Heft II (Roma: Pontificium Institutum Biblicum, 1953), p. 37.

[7]Cf. also Gen. 15:5.

[8]E.g., the length of Saul's reign as given by Paul in Acts 13:21. See Discussion on pp. 53, 54.

sums, but only with a rounded estimate of the total. This does not mean that the number is inaccurate and should be disregarded, but it should be interpreted in the light of the author's intentions for that number. The use of rounded numbers was not only common in ancient Israel, but was a much-used device in other lands which surrounded Israel. According to William Smith, an example of this use is found in the Moabite Stone.[9] In this inscription Mesha claims that Omri and Ahab occupied the area of Medeba for 40 years. The inscription reads as follows:

> Omri had occupied the land of Medeba, and (Israel) had dwelt in his time and half the time of his son (Ahab), forty years; but Chemosh dwelt there in my time.[10]

I Kings 16:23, 29, on the other hand, indicates this number should be about 23 years. If both of the reigns were counted in full, the total would only be 34 years. It seems strange that the scribe of the Moabite stone would round off the number 23 to 40. It would appear that 20 would be more accurate as a round number. Perhaps in this instance the writer was using the number in the sense of a generation, or that his reckoning was more inclusive than he indicates. Smith, on the basis of this inscription, concludes:

> . . . the number 40 must have been used very freely by Mesha's scribe as a round number. It is probably often used in that way in the Bible where it is remarkably frequent esp. in reference to period of days or years.[11]

It appears, however, that too much has been deduced from the meager and ambiguous information of the Mesha inscription. It does not follow conclusively that the Mesha stone in this place was definitely using 40 as a round number. Also, it is

---

[9]"Number," *The International Standard Bible Encyclopedia,* James Orr, ed. (Grand Rapids: Wm. B. Eerdmans Publishing Co., 1939), IV, p. 2158.

[10]W. F. Albright, trans., "Palestinian Inscriptions" *Ancient Near Eastern Texts Relating to the Old Testament,* James B. Pritchard, ed. (Princeton: Princeton University Press, 1955), p. 320.

[11]*Op. cit.,* p. 2158.

assuming too much to state that 40 could be used to represent
numbers as low as 23. It is quite true that the Bible uses the
number 40 many times, but one must examine the context and
the chronological data carefully to determine the manner in
which the writer is using that number. In some cases the number 40 is to be understood literally as representing exactly that
amount.[12] In other instances the number 40 can be regarded
as a rounded number representing a specific number near to it.
The Apostle Paul provides a good example of this usage in Acts
13:18, 20. The length of time God suffered their "manners" in
the wilderness is described as "about the time of forty years."
In verse 20 the apostle speaks of the time of the Judges as
"about the space of four hundred and fifty years." With the
introductory modifier *hōs* it is clear that the figures are only
rounded numbers. The Apostle's use of 40 is not always that
clear to discern, for in verse 21 of that chapter he gives the
reign of Saul as 40 years. This is the only place in the Bible
that the length of Saul's reign is given. Scholars are divided on
the significance of this number. Some argue that Paul was think-
ing in round numbers. They point out that he merely omitted
the qualifying expression *hōs*. Since the two previous numbers in
the context were rounded numbers it is reasonable to suppose
that this is the same. On the other hand, there are those who
feel the number 40 should be taken at its exact face value
numerically. It is argued that the omission of the word *hōs*
clearly indicates that the number was definite as distinguished
from the above numbers which were rounded.[13] I am inclined
to agree with the conclusion that:

> The question as to whether Paul meant to indicate that
> Saul occupied the throne exactly 40 years cannot be settled,
> and it does not affect the historical accuracy of the account.[14]

---

[12]Cf. Gen. 7:4, 17; 8:6; 25:20; 50:3; Num. 14:34; cf. also Acts 1:3;
7:23; etc.

[13]See Francis D. Nichol, ed., *The Seventh-day Adventist Bible Commentary* (Washington, D.C.; Review and Herald Publishing Association,
1954), II, pp. 131-132.

Cf. also the discussion of this problem in R. C. H. Lenski, *The Acts of
the Apostles* (Columbus, Ohio: The Wartburg Press, 1944), pp. 520, 521.

[14]Francis D. Nichol, ed., *Ibid.,* p. 132.

In the historical books the number 40 occurs with considerable regularity. The life of Moses is divided into three periods of forty years each (Acts 7:23; Exod. 7:7; Deut. 34:7), so also David (I Kings 2:11), Solomon (I Kings 11:42) and Jehoash (II Kings 12:1). The book of Judges contains many references to the number 40 (Judg. 3:11, 30; 5:31; 8:28; 13:10). With regard to the use of this number in the book of Judges, it will be seen that many critical scholars dismiss the number as symbolical and refuse to take it seriously:

> While such round numbers are not to be taken literally, this does not mean that all the other elements are unhistorical.[15]

There is no warrant for this conclusion, for while the numbers given may not represent exact amounts in every case, they are representations of an amount very close to them. There is no reason for regarding these numbers as other than actual representations of the amounts specified unless there is compelling evidence to do otherwise. It is admitted that because of the apparent schematic use of the number 40 (as well as 80 and 20) one should guard his conclusions carefully with regard to absolute dates for the period of the Judges.

Many of the larger numbers found in the Bible are rounded numbers. These numbers, like the smaller rounded numbers, are to be understood literally. The number 100 is sometimes used in this manner (e.g., Gen. 26:12; Lev. 26:8; II Sam. 24:3; Eccles. 8:12; Matt. 19:29). The number 1000 may sometimes refer to approximate amounts or an actual amount. In Genesis 20:16 and 35 ff. actual amounts of 1000 seem to be in view. Sometimes the number 1000 is employed to describe an indefinite amount as in Deuteronomy 1:11 and 7:9. The rounded use of 1000 (or 2000, 3000, etc.) is many times introduced by the expression "about." For example, in Exodus 32:28 we read "that there fell of the people that day about three thousand men" (Heb. kisloset 'alpê 'îs).[16]

---

[15]Cyrus H. Gordon, *World of the Old Testament* (New York: Doubleday & Company, Inc., 1958), pp. 151, 152.
[16]Cf. also Josh. 3:4; 4:13; 7:4; 8:12; etc.

B. Problems Relative to Conventional Numbers

The problem of large numbers.

Perhaps one of the greatest problems encountered in a study of the numbers of the Bible is the significance and reliability of large numbers. The highest numbers referred to in any way in the Bible are "a thousand thousand" (I Chron. 22:14; II Chron. 14:9), "thousands of thousands" (Dan. 7:10; Rev. 5:11) and twice that figure (Rev. 9:16). In many cases these numbers are used in a purely indefinite sense and therefore cause no interpretive problem. Large numbers that occur in a purely historical context sometimes raise problems even to the casual reader of Scripture. Gerald T. Kennedy's observation is pertinent:

> Larger numbers in the Bible have caused difficulties on two scores. First in certain sets of circumstances they seem impossible, and secondly, when one admits that a number seems to be used symbolically he does not have the key to the symbolism.[17]

The high numbers given for the size of the exodus (Num. 1, 26), the large number of men in David's census (1,300,000 in II Sam. 24:9, or 1,570,000 in I Chron. 21:5), the 7000 sheep sacrificed in Jerusalem (I Chron. 15:11), the large number of chariots used in the hill country (30,000 in I Sam. 13:5), the number who died in the punishment at Beth-shemesh (50,070 men, I Sam. 6:19) and many more such numbers have caused critics to suspect the historicity of the text. Smith's view is:

> That some of these high figures are incorrect is beyond reasonable doubt, and is not in the least surprising, for there is ample evidence that the numbers in ancient documents were exceptionally liable to corruption.[18]

This view is a fair representation of the majority of critical scholars who have expressed opinions on this subject. There is a large group of scholars who feel that these numbers are the

---

[17]"The Use of Numbers in Sacred Scripture," *American Ecclesiastical Review*, CXXXIX, No. 1, p. 30.

[18]*Op. cit.*, p. 2158.

result of the over active imagination of the writer.[19] Some large
numbers (e.g., the large number for the tribe of Judah in the
census lists of Num. 1, 26) can be accounted for by the politi-
cal-religious prejudice of the scribe, according to Gray.[20] But
such views should be challenged not only on the grounds of
their critical presuppositions,[21] but on the practicality of such a
proposition. It is highly questionable that these large numbers
would be impressive (to rival scribes of Judaic traditions, for
example) if they were as unrealistic as critics claim they were.
Who, in our age, would believe a news release which contends
that 200 people riding in a Volkswagen were killed in a high-
way accident traveling at a speed of 170 miles per hour? How
impressed would one be if a sea captain claimed that his 100
foot sailboat sank and 300,000 people lost their lives? The non-
sensical proposition that over-enthusiastic, religiously-oriented
scribes of certain tribes from later centuries changed the numbers of the Old Testament in order to make the story more
impressive must be firmly rejected as an insult to the intelligence, not only of the ancient Israelites, but to the modern
reader of Holy Scripture.

Antediluvian ages. One need not read far in the pages of the
Bible before he is confronted with large numbers which raise
serious questions. A case in point is the long lives of the
antediluvian patriarchs recorded in Genesis 5. According to
this chapter the average life span of these patriarchs, including
Enoch who was translated without dying at the age of 365, was
slightly over 857 years.

The customary treatment of this passage by many scholars is
to regard the whole narrative as mythical. The ages of the
antediluvian patriarchs is supposed, by some writers, to reflect

---

[19]Cf. George B. Gray, *Numbers, International Critical Commentary*
(New York: Charles Scribner's Sons, 1920), p. 14.

[20]*Ibid.* Cf. also Roland DeVaux, *Ancient Israel, Its Life and Institutions,*
Trans. John Mchugh (London: Darton, Longman & Todd, 1961), p. 65.

[21]According to Gray and others, the lists of Numbers 1 and 26 are the
work of P who copied from the earlier work of J,E. Cf. Gray, *op. cit.,* p.
14. Such propositions, based on an arbitrary literary analysis, are untenable
on several grounds. See John J. Davis, "The Patriarchs Knowledge of
Jehovah," *The Grace Journal,* IV (1963), No. 1, Winter.

epic traditions which may be traced back to Sumerian origins. Since the Sumerian antediluvian king list[22] enumerates kings who were supposed to have reigned for a total of 241,200 years, critics feel that the antediluvian longevity found in Genesis 5 is the result of borrowing on the part of the Hebrews. George A. Barton went to great length to prove that the Biblical material found in Genesis 5 had Sumerian origins. The names of the patriarchs found in the Bible were compared with the names in the Sumerian King list and it was claimed that striking similarities existed, thus supporting his contention.[23] The identifications which Barton attempted to establish, however, were strained and in some cases rather artificial.[24] Merrill F. Unger in his *Archaeology and the Old Testament* feels that:

> The value of the archaeological evidence in the case of original longevity does not lie in the conclusion that the Hebrews happened to hand down with more restraint than the Babylonians the primitive traditions of the original stock of which both peoples were descendants. There is no valid reason why they should have done so. The manifest soberness of the Hebrew account is an indication of its inspiration as divine truth. The Babylonian lists are illuminating as representing an independent and confirmatory, though grossly exaggerated, tradition of that which appears in Genesis 5 as authentic historical fact given by divine revelation.[25]

There is no reason for rejecting the ages of the antediluvian patriarchs as both unreasonable and impossible. The drastic drop in longevity may be explained on sound scientific grounds,[26] and it may have been due to God's judicial dealing with mankind in the flood. H. C. Leupold argues that:

---

[22]The Sumerian king list was probably written in the Third Dynasty of Ur or earlier. See Jack Finegan, *Light From the Ancient Past* (Princeton: Princeton University Press, 1959), p. 29.

[23]*Archaeology and the Bible* (Philadelphia: American Sunday-school Union, 1916), p. 317 ff.

[24]Note his attempt to equate Abel of Gen. 4 with SIBA LU of the Sumerian King list. *Op. cit.*, p. 326.

[25](Grand Rapids: Zondervan Publishing House, 1954), p. 19.

[26]John C. Whitcomb and Henry M. Morris, *The Genesis Flood* (Philadelphia: The Presbyterian and Reformed Publishing Co., 1961), p. 404.

> He . . . who is duly impressed by the excellence of man's
> original estate, will have no difficulty in accepting the com-
> mon explanation that even under the curse of sin man's con-
> stitution displayed such vitality that it did not at first submit
> to the ravages of time until after centuries had passed.[27]

The most common method of escaping the problem connected
with these large numbers is to make "year" mean a shorter
period such as a month. This view, however, finds no support
at all in the Biblical text for the term "year" is never used in this
manner in the Old Testament. In addition to this textual weakness, there is a serious chronological problem that is raised by
such a view. In Genesis 5:6 we are told that Seth begat Enos
when he was 105 years old. If "years" in this text really means
"months" then this verse would propose that Seth had a son
when he was only about nine years old! This is impossible for
the Scriptures would then be suggesting a scientific impossibility
as well as a chronological absurdity. It appears that the most
sensible approach to the numbers found in Genesis 5 is to accept
them as real and representing a biological-climatical phenomenon which we are incapable of witnessing today.

Size of the exodus. According to Exodus 12:37, Numbers 1
and 26 the approximate size of the fighting force organized during the exodus and wandering was about 603,000 men. This census includes only males over the age of twenty years (who were
able to go to war, Num. 1:3). Gray observes that:

> Males over twenty form but a little more than a quarter of
> a whole population, thus (neglecting the 51,000 odd Levites)
> the total in chapter 1 (603,550) represents a total of men,
> women and children well exceeding 2,000,000.[28]

He further comments on these numbers as follows: "These numbers must on every ground be regarded as entirely unhistorical
and unreal. . . ."[29] The opinion that the numbers presented in

---

[27]*Exposition of Genesis* (Grand Rapids: Baker Book House, 1958), p. 234.
[28]*Op. cit.*, p. 12.
[29]*Ibid.* p. 11.

Exodus 12:37, Numbers 1 and 26 are impossible and unreal is shared by most critical scholars.[30]

There are a number of reasons given by these scholars why the numbers of the exodus should be discounted as unrealistic. The first argument is that it would be impossible, naturally, for that many people to cross the Red Sea in the short time indicated. The answer to this problem is found, first of all, in the fact that the parting of the Red Sea was not merely a natural phenomenon.[31] Furthermore, Robinson in his *Researches in Palestine* showed that such a crossing was possible in a short period of time even though two million people would have been involved:

> As the Israelites numbered more than two millions of persons, besides flocks and herds, they would of course be able to pass but slowly. If the part left dry were broad enough to enable them to cross in a body one thousand abreast, which would require a space of more than half a mile in breadth (and is perhaps the largest supposition admissible), still the column would be more than two thousand persons in depth, and in all probability could not have extended less than two miles. It would then have occupied at least an hour in passing over its own length, or in entering the sea; and deducting this from the largest time intervening, before the Egyptians also have entered the sea, there will remain only time enough, under the circumstances, for the body of the Israelites to have passed at the most, over a space of three or four miles.[32]

It is therefore evident, that if proper conditions did exist, such a crossing would be possible. As to the probability of such an

---

[30]See W. M. Flinders Petrie, *Researches in Sinai* (London: Hazell, Watson and Viney, Ltd., 1906), p. 207 f.

R. E. D. Clark, "The Large Numbers of the Old Testament," *Journal of the Transactions of the Victoria Institute,* Vol. 87.

Roland DeVaux, *op. cit.,* p. 65.

S. R. Driver, *The Book of Exodus* (Cambridge: The University Press, 1953), p. 101.

[31]C. F. Keil and F. Delitzsch, *Biblical Commentary on the Old Testament,* Trans. James Martin (Grand Rapids: Wm. B. Eerdmans Publishing Co., 1949), II, p. 47.

[32]Quoted in Keil and Delitzsch, *Ibid.,* p. 47.

event taking place, one must by faith accept the simple statements of Scripture.

The second objection to the large numbers of the exodus is
that the desert area of the Sinai peninsula would be incapable
of supporting that many people. Petrie argues:

> We see, then, that by the general condition of the small water
> supply on the road and at the wells, and by this crucial case
> of an almost drawn battle against some 5,000 people — we
> cannot suppose that the Israelites were much more than this
> number [i.e., 5000-6000].[33]

This argument completely overlooks the supernatural provi-
sions of food and water. Manna was supplied every day (Exod.
16) and when the occasion demanded it, water was provided
(Exod. 15:23-26; 17:5-7; Num. 20:7-12). There were occasions
when quail were provided by God to meet the needs of the
people and this was done on a large scale (Exod. 16:13; Num.
11:31, 32; cf. Ps. 105:40).

In addition to the food God provided, there seem to be some
indications in Scripture that God also provided rain during the
exodus thus increasing, at least for a short time, the fertility and
productivity of the land. Psalm 68:7-9 reads as follows in the
A.S.V.:

> 7. O God, when thou wentest forth before thy people,
>   When thou didst march through the wilderness;
> 8. The earth trembled, the heavens also dropped rain at the
>   presence of God.
>   Yon Sinai trembled at the presence of God, the God of
>   Israel.
> 9. Thou, O God, didst send a plentiful rain
>   Thou didst confirm thine inheritance, when it was weary.

In verse 8 the expression "the heavens also dropped" is 'ap šāma-
yim nāṭepû. The verb nāṭepû, "dropped" (from nātap), has the
idea of "discharging drops, to rain."[34] In the victory song of

---

[33]Op. cit., pp. 207-208 (brackets mine).
[34]Joseph A. Alexander, *The Psalms Translated and Explained* (Grand
Rapids: Zondervan Publishing House, n.d.), p. 285.

Deborah in Judges 5 the same verb form occurs and the significance of the expression is quite clear. Verse 4 (ASV) of that
chapter reads:

> Jehovah, when thou sentest forth out of Seir,
> When thou marchedst out of the field of Edom,
> The earth trembled, the heavens also dropped,
> Yea, the clouds dropped water.

If there were a temporary increase in rainfall, this would have
provided enough water to meet basic dietary needs as well as
provided limited irrigation for crops. The Israelites, according to
Albright, were able to survive and grow in the hill countries of
Palestine later principally because they had developed the art of
cistern construction.

> . . . Israelite population increased rapidly in the hills. Thanks
> to the rapid spread of the art, then recent, of constructing
> cisterns and lining them with waterproof lime plaster instead
> of the previously used limy marl or raw-lime plaster, the Is-
> raelites were able to settle in any site where there was rain,
> whereas their earlier Canaanite precursors had been forced to
> restrict their occupation in general to sites near springs or peren-
> nial springs.[35]

It might be that the art of constructing such cisterns was
developed in the desert when the preservation of rain was an
absolute necessity.[36] Some argue to some length for the
uniqueness of the wilderness journey and the possibility of a
somewhat different climatic and agricultural situation, but most
of their propositions are rather speculative.[37]

The third objection, which was raised first by Petrie[38] and

---

[35]*The Archaeology of Palestine* (Baltimore: Penguin Books, 1961), p. 113.

[36]It should be observed, however, that this is speculative since there is minimal evidence for the existence of many Late Bronze II-Iron I cisterns of this type in the desert areas. This unique art could have been acquired in Palestine itself, although the evidence seems to support the idea that Israel brought the practice with them into the land.

[37]*Numbers, Commentary on the Holy Scriptures*, ed. by John P. Lange and Philip Schaff (Grand Rapids: Zondervan Publishing House, n.d.), p. 12 ff.

[38]*Op. cit.*, p. 214.

then adopted by Clark,[39] is that it would be impossible for Moses to have judged two million alone (cf. Exod. 18:13-17). Petrie argued that by reducing the population to 5000 or 6000 the statements in Exodus would not seem unreasonable.[40] The text in Exodus does not say, however, that Moses successfully judged all the people but just that he was the only judge at that time and was confronted with people from morning to night (Exod. 18:13, 14). In fact, Jethro clearly indicates that the task Moses had assumed was an impossible one (vs. 18) and suggests that judges be selected for the thousands, hundreds, fifties, and tens (vs. 21 f.).[41]

The fourth objection to the large numbers of the exodus is the fact that Israel could be refused passage through a small portion of land by a rather insignificant people and appear to have great difficulty in taking Canaan in spite of their large numbers. Petrie alludes to this situation in his *Researches in Sinai.*[42]

With regard to the refusal of the Edomites to allow the Israelites to pass through the land John Rea observes:

> . . . it must be recognized that on the basis of the passage in Num. 20:14-21 the Edomites were a fairly numerous and strong people at the time when they refused Moses's request (verses 20, 21). On the other hand, they need not have been nearly so strong as the Israelites, because God commanded Moses to say to the people: "They will be afraid of you: take heed unto yourselves therefore: contend not with them; for I will not give you of their land . . . because I have given

[39]*Op. cit.,* p. 86.

[40]*Op. cit.,* p. 214.

[41]The breakdown here is most interesting and enlightening. It seems to imply that the numerical composition of the company of people involved thousands and many smaller units. This mitigates against a view that 'elep means family or tribe in the census lists. If 'elep means "tent" or "family" what could "fifty" "hundred" or "ten" possibly mean? The "tent" or "family" is normally the smallest unit among nomadic and semi-nomadic peoples. This breakdown also occurs in the Dead Sea Scrolls. See Theodor H. Gaster, *The Dead Sea Scriptures in English Translation* (Garden City, New York: Doubleday Anchor Books, 1956), pp. 42, 81.

[42]P. 207.

mount Seir unto Esau for a possession" (Deut. 2:4b, 5). It was a combination, then, of the Edomites' stubbornness to grant permission to cross their territory and of God's sovereign plan that Israel should settle in Canaan that caused the Jews to go around Edom.[43]

A more difficult problem is that of the population of Canaan itself. It appears to some that the Joshua-Judges narratives indicate that Israel carried out with considerable difficulty the conquest of the land which should not be the case if they numbered over two million. Estimations, however, of the population of Palestine at the time of the exodus vary and are difficult to support since insufficient evidence must be relied on. Edward F. Campbell's estimation of the population of Palestine in the Amarna period is that it was rather small.

> . . . the population in Palestine, and especially in the hill country, must have been very small. One estimate suggests 200,000 for all Palestine, about 20,000 to 25,000 for all the wooded central hill country.[44]

Other estimates range from two hundred thousand to one million. For the most part estimates tend to depend on recent population figures. Herman Guthe provided the following information:

> The present area of Palestine . . . is estimated at over 9,000 square miles, with an approximate population of 559,127. This population was doubtless larger during the centuries of Roman control and the early period of Arab dominion, probably the happiest ages of Palestine. In still earlier ages, however, it is improbable that the population was much greater than at present.[45]

---

[43]*"The Historical Setting of the Exodus and Conquest"* (Winona Lake: Grace Theological Seminary, 1958 Unpublished ThD dissertation), pp. 184, 185.

[44]"The Amarna Letters and the Amarna Period," *The Biblical Archaeologist*, Vol. 23 (Feb. 1960), p. 21.

[45]"Palestine," *The New Schaff-Herzog Encyclopedia of Religious Knowledge*, Samuel M. Jackson, ed. (Grand Rapids: Baker Book House, 1950), p. 319.

DeVaux argues that in the eighth century B.C. "the total population of Israel and Judah cannot have been much more than one million."[46] He further observes:

> By way of comparison, we may note that at the British census of 1931, before the great Zionist immigration, Palestine had 1,914,000 inhabitants. It is questionable whether the country could ever have supported many more people in ancient times without the assistance of those artificial resources which modern economy provides.[47]

Along with the problem of the Canaanite population of Canaan is the question as to whether the land of Palestine would have been capable of supporting some two million Israelites along with the native population. There is no doubt that the area to be occupied was relatively small. The average breadth was not over 50 miles and the length "from Dan to Beersheba" was approximately 150 miles. Excluding the areas inhabited by the Philistines and Phoenicians (500 square miles) there was approximately 7000 square miles of land for Israel.[48] This would mean that there would be about 285 inhabitants per square mile. This figure is not unreasonable according to Thompson because the density of population has been paralleled and exceeded elsewhere:

> Belgium has about three hundred and thirty, North Holland four hundred and fifty-five, and South Holland four hundred and sixty-nine inhabitants to the square mile.[49]

He further argues that settlement of that many people is not impossible because:

> . . . it is a fact not contested, I believe, that the mode of living in ancient times was much simpler than now, and hence

---

[46]*Op. cit.,* p. 67. Edersheim regards a population for Israel of 5 to 6 million as not execessive. *Bible History of the Old Testament* (Grand Rapids: Baker Book House, reprint, 1949), II, p. 40.

[47]*Ibid.,* p. 67.

[48]William M. Thompson, *The Land and the Book* (New York: Harper & Brothers Publishers, 1908), I, p. 98.

[49]William M. Thompson, *Ibid.*

much less was required to maintain an individual then than at present.[50]

It appears, therefore, that at least statistically one is able to show the possibility of such large numbers of people occupying ancient Palestine.

There are a number of other ways of handling this problem which only require careful consideration of the Biblical data. In the first place, it appears that it is rather dangerous to depend on modern day density statistics as a guideline for determining population figures of the fifteenth or fourteenth centuries B.C. Political and topographical changes would have changed population statistics in Palestine as it has in every land. Palestine, perhaps as no other land, has undergone many such changes. It is clear from the Old Testament that the condition of the land was quite different from that which we see today. In ancient times the land was forested in many areas which would provide better soil conservation. Over the years most trees have been removed from the hills causing serious erosion and loss of fertile soil. In addition to this, the land at the time of the conquest was heavily populated with wild life of all kinds.[51] If such animals were in abundance and if the land were better forested as the Scriptures seem to indicate, it is not hard to suppose a total population of Palestine of two to five million at the time of the conquest.

In the second place, it does not follow that because Israel numbered some two million people they were militarily superior. In fact, if the record of the oppression is true, we should expect some military difficiency among the fleeing Israelites. With regard to the conquest of Canaan, it should be remembered that it was a whole new generation that entered with Joshua and perhaps with minimal fighting experience. Whatever experience the Israelite armies had in fighting, it would not have equipped them to cope with the sophisticated chariot war-

---

[50]*Ibid.*

[51]Deut. 7:22 indicates that God drove out the nations "little by little: thou mayest not consume them at once, lest the beasts of the field increase upon thee." This would seem to indicate an abundance of wild life.

fare of the Canaanites. In fact, on several occasions the Bible plainly states that this was one reason why some of the tribes were not successful in conquest.[52] Israel, as a fighting force, could only be successful if their military ventures were subjected to a godly faith and obedience.

In the third place, because Israel had a fighting force of over 600,000 men does not mean that all the men would have, or could have been used in a given battle. This is why Joshua, for the most part, fought with military units numbering only 10,000 to 40,000,[53] for in the hill country of eastern Palestine any more men than that number would be a detriment rather than an asset. Beside this consideration, it was probably the plan of God that Israel not use large forces with which to fight lest they attribute victory to their power rather than the power of God. G. Ernest Wright attempts to show that an army of 600,000 had no reason to fear the Pharaoh of Egypt for he could not match that size an army.

> In the greatest battle of his career, that against the Hittites at Kadesh in Syria, Pharaoh Rameses II had an army of four divisions, totaling scarcely more than 20,000 men. If the figures in the book of Numbers, therefore, really represented the actual number involved in the exodus, the Israelite army of 600,000 warriors should have been able to overcome anything which the Pharaoh put into the field by sheer weight of numbers.[54]

There are three weaknesses in this argument. First, he assumes that Ramses II was in power at the time of the exodus which is in conflict with clear Biblical data, which places the exodus in the middle of the fifteenth century B.C. during the reign of the Thutmosides.[55] In the second place, it seems

---

[52]Cf. Judg. 1:19, 4:3; Josh. 17:16. Although this was not a valid excuse because they were given impressive victories over chariot forces (Josh. 11 and Judg. 4, 5). It was disobedience and unbelief that spelled defeat.

[53]Cf. Josh. 7:3; 8:3, 12.

[54]Biblical Archaeology (Philadelphia: The Westminister Press, 1957), p. 66.

[55]I Kings 6:1 states that the exodus took place 480 years before the fourth year of Solomon. The fourth year of Solomon is 967/66 B.C. which would place the exodus about the year 1446/45 B.C. Note also the chronological implications of Jephthah's statement in Judg. 11:26.

rather strange to suppose that the size of the army of the
Pharaoh in a given battle, far in the north, would represent the
total national military potential of Egypt. In the third place, it
is very doubtful that 600,000[56] soldiers, untrained and un-
equipped could defeat "by sheer numbers" a well-equipped,
well-disciplined army of one of the greatest powers of the
Near East at that time.

The meaning of 'elep ("thousand"). It has been shown that
among critical scholars there is general agreement that the
number of people involved in the exodus is both unreal and
impossible. In view of this assumption several alternative explanations have been given for the significance of the numbers
of Numbers 1 and 26. Most explanations revolve around the
meaning of the term *'elep* usually translated "thousand." George
E. Mendenhall observes that:

> There seems to be a consensus among those who have treated
> the census lists in the Book of Numbers since 1903 on at
> least two points; first, that the word *'elep* does not mean "thou-
> sand" but rather is a designation of some subsection of a tribe;
> and second, that the numbers are impossible.[57]

One of the earliest attempts to interpret *'elep* other than "thousand" was that of W. M. Flinders Petrie. He attempted to establish the fact that the "hundreds" in the list were independent
designations from the thousands. He observed that there was
not a single round thousand in the list, there was not a single
100, 800, or 900; and that the greater part of the numbers fell
on 400 or 500. By arranging the census lists in ascending numerical order, then separating the hundreds and organizing
them in single digits, he arrived at the following symmetrical pattern which he claimed was ". . . overwhelming evidence that
the hundreds have . . . an origin entirely independent of the
thousands."[58]

---

[56]It will be shown later that this figure and others like it represent primarily military potential and not a mobilized army (cf. pp. 79, 80).

[57]"The Census Lists of Numbers 1 and 26," *Journal of Biblical Literature,*
LXXVII (March, 1958), p. 52.

[58]*Op. cit.,* p. 210.

				4	5				
				4	5				
				4	5				
				4	5				
				4	5	6	7		
		2	3	4	5	6	7		
		2	3	4	5	6	7		
	none							none	
digit	0	1	2	3	4	5	6	7	8	9

He concluded that the expression 32,200, as it reads normally, actually means 32 families, 200 people. This assumption, of course, is based on the premise that 'elep here means "group" or "family." From this he developed the idea that term 'elep meant "tents" and the number of Manasseh, for example, was not 32,200 but 32 tents for 200 people. In chart form his scheme works out as follows:[59]

	Numbers 1			Numbers 26		
	Tents	Nos.	Per tent	Tents	Nos.	Per tent
Reuben	46	500	9	43	730	17
Simeon	59	300	5	22	200	9
Gad	45	650	14	40	500	12
Judah	74	600	8	76	500	7
Issachar	54	400	7	64	300	5
Zebulun	57	400	7	60	500	8
Ephraim	40	500	12	32	500	16
Manasseh	32	200	6	52	700	13
Benjamin	35	400	11	45	600	13
Dan	62	700	11	64	400	6
Asher	41	500	12	53	400	8
Naphtali	53	400	8	45	400	9
	598	5,550	93	596	5,730	96

[59]*Ibid.*, p. 211.

According to his view, therefore, the total number of people involved in the exodus would not be two million or more, but 5,550 at the beginning and 5,730 after thirty-eight years.

This view had appeal to some, but on the whole it has not gained wide acceptance even among critical scholars. Most reject this proposition because it has little support from the Hebrew.[60] R. E. D. Clark rejects the view and says "to read 'families' in place of 'thousands' in many of the other texts can scarcely be said to improve the sense."[61] If there were only 5000 to 6000 people involved in the exodus, the words of the Pharaoh in Exodus 1:8 were strange indeed. Whether the "king who knew not Joseph" was a Hyksos king or native Egyptian it is unlikely that the Israelites would be "more and mightier." Also, it appears that Petrie overlooks the fact that this is a military census and this being so, the population would not be 5000 to 6000 but 20,000 to 24,000, assuming that males over twenty constitute little more than a quarter of a total population.[62] The final weakness of this theory is the fact that the Book of Numbers gives the totals of the census and these totals are based on the grammatical assumption that 'elep means "thousand." Numbers 1:46 and 2:32 gives the totals of the first census as 603,550 men and Numbers 26:51 the second census as being 601,730.

In 1955 Clark presented a paper to the Victoria Institute in England proposing that the term 'elep should be read as "captains" or "mighty men."[63] For Reuben he would read not 46,500 but 46 officers plus 500 men. This view, like that of Petrie, contains serious weaknesses. In the first place, this interpretation of 'elep cannot be applied consistently elsewhere. In Numbers 31:32-40 it would be impossible to make 'elep "captain" or "mighty men." In I Samuel 6:19 and I Kings 20:30 the term 'iš is used with 'elep and would thus appear to rule out

[60]George E. Wright, op. cit., p. 67.

[61]"The Large Numbers of the Old Testament," Journal of the Transactions of the Victoria Institute, LXXXVII (1955), p. 84. We shall show later that what Clark said of Petrie's view can be said of his own, infra., p. 70 ff.

[62]Supra, p. 58.

[63]Op. cit., p. 84.

the theory of Clark. In the second place, Clark appears to be making the common mistake of deducing the meaning of a word from its etymology, according to which *'alluph* should mean leader, instead of asking how it is actually used. In the third place, the Hebrew has a good word for officer which is *śar*. Donald J. Wiseman makes some pertinent observations on the etymology of *'lp* and raises some interesting questions with regard to Clark's propositions:

> Basically the Hebrew root *'lp* seems to mean "to be familiar with" and is used in this sense in Proverbs 22:25, Job 15:5, 33:33, 35:11 [A.V. "learn, teach"]; and frequently as an adjective [A.V. "tame" e.g., Jeremiah 11:19]. The word parallels *meyuda'* ["friend" i.e., one with whom one is familiar]. In ancient Near Eastern texts a man who had special knowledge being familiar with some art whether of peace of war, was *ipso facto* a leader. Hence the Hebrew *'alluph* [literally, "one who has learned, become familiar with . . ."] is the "chief" or "leader" [Gen. 36:15 *et passim*]. There may be some connection here with the Hebrew *'eleph* ["cattle," cf. the Accadian *alpu* used of large horned beasts, etc.] which is the word used to describe the first or leading sign of the *alp*habet derived from the Phoenician pictogram of a horned beast . . . Could the Hebrew *'lp* mean simply "trained [regular?] soldier" as much as the Accadian *ummanu* ["expert"] is used in the collective plural for "army" (*ummanati*)?[64]

It should also be observed that if one supports this view he must allow for a rather loose, individualistic military organization. Note for example that Simeon would have 59 "captains" over 300 men (Num. 1:23) while God would have 45 "captains" over 650 men (Num. 1:25). It is rather strange indeed that there would be such an inconsistent captain-unit ratio between the tribes.

In answer to this view it should also be noted that in Exodus 38:26 we are told that every male of Israel over twenty years of age gave a half-shekel when a census was taken. The total silver collected agrees with the figure of 603,550 in Numbers 1. The interpretation of *'elep* as "captain" by Clark raises a num-

---

ber of serious textual problems. For example Gideon started out with an army of 32 "captains" (*'elapîm*) according to Clark's view (Judges 7:3). Twenty-two "captains" (*'elep*) returned leaving him with only ten "captains" (*'elapîm*). But in Judges 7:4 we are told that there were too many people! In addition to that, Judges 7:6 indicates that after a special test 300 men remained and that is strange indeed if only ten "captains" were sent to the water!

An even more serious problem is raised by the record of the failure of the Israelite army to take Ai on the first attempt (Joshua 7). Joshua sent up 2 or 3 (*'elep*) "captains" but we are told in verse 5 that 36 men died![65]

A more recent attempt to solve the problem of the large numbers in the census lists of Numbers is that of George Mendenhall in the *Journal of Biblical Literature*.[66] The basis for his view is essentially that of Petrie and Clark, namely that *'elep* does not mean "thousand" but some unit or group. He argues that the military character of the army recorded in Numbers is that of the Federation (i.e., the Judges) period. He remarks:

> It is here submitted that the census lists of Numbers 1 and 26 are an authentic list from the period of the Federation which reflects this sort of military organization and mobilization, probably coming from specific occasions when the Federation army had to mobilize to meet a common peril. Consequently, the lists cannot be taken to be a complete total of all men of fighting age, but are rather a list of the contingents sent to war by each of the tribes, similar to the lists found in the *Iliad*.[67]

It is apparent that his historical analysis of the social-political structure of Israel for the exodus period is that of Martin Noth. He assumes, along with Noth, that the ". . . the largest socio-

---

[65]According to Clark's method, the population in the wilderness would total 140,000 instead of 2-3 million. This figure is still unacceptable to many commentators because it is too large. For a recent discussion of this point see J. W. Wenham, "Large Numbers in the Old Testament," *Tyndale Bulletin* (London: Tyndale Press, 1967), p. 31.

[66]Mendenhall, *loc. cit.*

[67]*Ibid.*, p. 60.

political unit in ancient Israel was the 'tribe!' "[68] Military readiness was more after the pattern of a "folk militia" rather than a standing army.[69] The census lists of Numbers, therefore, represent tribal divisions rather than a general military census of all males of military age. He comments:

> The census lists then consist of an enumeration of the number of units ('alafim) into which each tribe is subdivided, and following that, the total number of men to be levied from the tribe.[70]

According to this analysis, the census list of Numbers 1 would yield the following results:

Tribe	Units	Men
Reuben	46	500
Simeon	59	300
Gad	45	650
Judah	74	600
Issachar	54	400
Zebulun	57	400
Ephraim	40	500
Manasseh	32	200
Benjamin	35	400
Dan	62	700
Asher	41	500
Naphtali	53	400
	598	5550

It will be observed that this analysis produces the same results as that of Petrie's method.[71]

This view, like that of Petrie and Clark, suffers from several logical and Biblical weaknesses. First, he assumes that these numbers belong to the Federation period rather than the Mosaic

---

[68]*Ibid.*, p. 54. Cf. Martin Noth, *The History of Israel* (New York: Harper & Row, second edition, 1960), p. 85 ff.

[69]*Ibid.*, p. 57.

[70]*Ibid.*, p. 61.

[71]*Supra.* pp. 68, 69.

era, an assumption which is purely arbitrary.[72] In the second place, it does not follow that the military organization of Israel during the wilderness journey had to be like that of the Federation. The political, geographical and cultural situation of the exodus was quite different from that of the settlement. In the third place, he, like other writers who contend for a reinterpretation of 'elep, completely ignores the totals of the census given in Numbers 1:46, 2:32 and 26:51.[73]

There does not seem to be any sufficient reason for rejecting the normal interpretation of the numbers given in the census lists of Numbers 1 and 26. It is admittedly difficult to conceive of such a vast number of people moving through the desert areas of Sinai, but this does not rule out the possibility of such an event taking place. Scholars have not dismissed the large numbers of the exodus because archaeological or topographical data would absolutely forbid it, but because such a vast number of people would require supernatural assistance which *a priori*, they reject.

There are times in the Hebrew text of the Old Testament when 'elep does mean "family" or "tribe." The following examples demonstrate this usage:

1. Judges 6:15 "My family (*'alpî*) is poor in Manasseh."[74]

2. Micah 5:2 "But thou, Beth-lehem Ephrathah, which art little to be among the thousands (*be'alpēy*) of Judah."

3. Numbers 1:16 "They are the heads of the thousands (*'alpê*) of Israel."

4. I Sam. 10:19 "Present yourselves before the Lord by your tribes and by your thousands (*le'alpêkem*).

Several observations should be made concerning the above uses of 'elep. In most cases the immediate context indicates the value of 'elep when military units are not under considera-

---

[72]Cf. Mendenhall, *op. cit.*, p. 55 ff.

[73]In addition to these texts is Num. 11:21 which gives the rounded total of 600,000 footmen.

[74]This statement might have reference to a military unit as Mendenhall contends, *op. cit.*, p. 60.

tion. It should be noted that no other number is used with *'elep* in these texts. This seems to indicate an idiomatic employment of the term. A parallel to this syntactical phenomenon is the word *yom* "day." In some texts it is used alone without a numerical adjective and in that situation may refer to a literal day or an indefinite period of time (e.g., Gen. 2:4). But when a numerical adjective is used with this term and the context reveals chronological sequence the word day usually refers to a normal 24 hour solar period.[75] It seems that when *'elep* is used in contexts other than census lists or military enumerations and has no additional numerical values attached, it might have idiomatic significance (e.g., "tribe, family, military, unit"). The precise significance must be determined by the context alone. Normally, however, the term is most naturally understood in its general usage as a mathematical designation of a quantity and this is especially true in historical narratives involving military statistics.

Conclusions on the size of the exodus. It is the view of this writer that numbers presented in the historical narratives describing the exodus from Egypt are both reliable and credible. One would be highly suspicious of the continuous emphasis of the exodus story in the page of Holy Writ if there were only a couple of tribes involved numbering 5000 to 6000 people. The size of this great event and the multiplied examples of the miraculous provision of God for His people make this the highlight of Israel's history. All are agreed that if one holds to the credibility of the numbers as they stand in Exodus and Numbers, he must rely on the miraculous preservation and sustaining power of God to make the accounts feasible.[76]

When one considers the long period of time associated with the oppression (c. 400 years) in Egypt, and the statements made concerning the size and might of Israel prior to the exodus (Exod. 1), it is not at all unreasonable to regard the size of the nation as approximately two million. It is difficult to see how

---

[75]Cf. Gen. 1 and Num. 7. For further discussion of this problem see E. J. Young, *Studies in Genesis One* (Philadelphia: Presbyterian and Reformed Publishing Co., 1964), p. 43 ff.

[76]Cf. A. A. MacRae, "Numbers" *The New Bible Commentary* (Grand Rapids: Wm. B. Eerdmans Publishing Co., 1963), p. 165.

a total population of 5000 could make a significant impression on Canaan, let alone gain mention on the Mernepta stela.[77]

It seems rather impossible to interpret the term 'elep as meaning "tribe," "family," or "military unit," in the census lists on Numbers in the light of the following facts:

1. Most of the numerals include hundreds as well as thousands.

2. The tribe of Gad numbered 42,650 (Num. 1:25) indicating a three-fold numerical declension i.e., thousands, hundreds, and fifties (cf. Exod. 18:21).

3. The totals are given for the census and they were added up on the basis of 'elep meaning "thousand" not "tribe" or "military unit" (Num. 1:46; 2:32; 26:51).

Differences between the census lists. Between the first census taken at the beginning of the journey and the census just before entrance into Canaan, many rather significant and catastrophic events took place among the children of Israel. The unusual nature of these events is reflected in the increases and decreases in the two census lists (see Table No. 5, p. 76). Dan, for example, increased 1700, Zebulun 3100, Issachar 9900, Benjamin 10,200, Asher 11,900, Manasseh 20,500, and Judah 1900. The increases range from 19 per cent in the case of Issachar to 63 per cent in the case of Manasseh. The increase of Manasseh in the short period of thirty-eight years seems impossible but it is not without parallel.

> The total population of Prussia increased from 10,349,031 to 17,139,288 between the end of 1816 and the end of 1855, that is to say, more than 65 per cent in 39 years; whilst in England the population increased 47 per cent between 1815 and 1849, i.e., in 34 years.[78]

At the same time there were some significant decreases such as in the tribe of Simeon where there were 37,100 less. Decreases are seen in the tribe of Reuben 2770, Gad 5150, Ephraim 8000, and Naphtali 8000. The decreases are probably accounted for in the history of the period itself. Lange remarks:

---

[77]Cf. *ANET.* p. 376, 378. It is not certain, however, that all peoples listed on this stela were numerous. With limited data we only assume this to be the case for many of them.

[78]Keil and Delitzsch, *op. cit.*, Vol. III, p. 8.

The decrease in the total during a period in which a marked
increase might justly have been looked for, corresponds with
the history of Israel in the wilderness, and the many great
catastrophes that were decreed against the people.[79]

The rather large losses sustained by the tribe of Simeon might
be accounted for in the sin and judgment at Baal Peor
(Num. 25). One of the men that was slain was Zimri "a prince
of a chief house among the Simeonites" (Num. 25:14). It is
usually conjectured, on the basis of the information in this
verse, that Simeon was perhaps the largest participant in the
sin at that place and therefore suffered the greatest losses. According to Numbers 25:9 some 24,000 died as a result of their
sin. Numbers 26:9, 10 seems to indicate that the tribe of Reuben
was very much reduced by the fate of the company of Korah.

TABLE 5

THE TWO NUMBERINGS[80]

Tribe	Before Wanderings	After Wanderings	Gains	Losses
Reuben	46,500	43,730		2,770
Simeon	59,300	22,200		37,100
Gad	46,650	40,500		5,150
Judah	74,600	76,500	1,900	
Issachar	54,400	64,300	9,900	
Zebulun	57,400	60,500	3,100	
Ephraim	40,500	32,500		8,000
Manasseh	32,200	52,700	20,500	
Benjamin	35,400	45,600	10,200	
Dan	62,700	64,400	1,700	
Asher	41,500	53,400	11,900	
Naphtali	53,400	45,400		8,000
	603,550	601,730	59,200	61,020

[79]*Op. cit.*, p. 11.
[80]Num. 1, 26.

The size of the tribe of Levi. According to the first census of Levi taken in the second year of the journey (Num. 3:39) they numbered 22,000 males of a month old and upwards; while in the census taken in the fortieth year (Num. 26:62) they numbered only 23,000. The increase shown in these figures is extremely low and has been the subject of considerable criticism from liberals. But according to Keil and Delitzsch these figures should not be questioned because they are perfectly reasonable.

> . . . the correctness of the numbers given is not to be called into question. It is not only supported by the fact, that the number of Levites capable of service between the ages of 30 and 50 amounted to 8580 (chap. iv:48), — a number which bears the most proportion to that of 22,000 of a month old and upwards, — but is also confirmed by the fact, that in the time of David the tribe of Levi only numbered 38,000 of thirty years old and upwards (I Chron. xxiii:3)[81]

The reason for the minimal increase is probably found in the fact that Levi, like many of the other tribes, suffered the judgment of God on several occasions.

> It is mentioned expressly that the sons of Aaron, Nadab and Abihu, died childless (chap. 3:4), and the stress put upon the fact that the children of Korah were not destroyed with their father (chap. 26:11), points directly to the implied antithesis, that after all, many levites did perish in the conspiracy of Korah.[82]

Petrie was faced with somewhat of a dilemma when he attempted to interpret the numbers given for the Levites. He would not accept the numbers at face value because this would suppose that only one man in thirteen had any children since there were only 22,273 first-born to 603,500 men.[83] On the other hand, he could not read *'elep̱* as "families" for that would yield equally unacceptable results. He concluded that the census of

---

[81]*Op. cit.*, Vol. III, p. 9.
[82]Lange, *loc. cit.*
[83]*Op. cit.*, p. 215.

the Levites was taken sometime after the conquest and did not represent data belonging to the exodus story. He argues:

> There was, then, no tribe of Levi at the time of the census, but it was created as a priestly caste at a later age.[84]

The conclusion of Petrie at this point appears to be rather subjective and arbitrary. In addition to this, it is in direct conflict with evidence that all the tribes, including the Levites, participated in the exodus (cf. Exod. 1:2; 6:16; 38:21).

The firstborn among the tribes. One of the more perplexing problems encountered in the book of Numbers is the total of firstborn among the tribes. According to the census taken for the purpose of redemption, all the male firstborn of the twelve tribes totaled only 22,273. If the nation had a population of more than a million males, which would probably be the case if there were 603,550 men of twenty years old and upwards, then on the assumption that 22,273 represents the sum total of all firstborn in the nation, there would only be one firstborn to forty or fifty males. This implies that every father of a family must have begotten, or still had, thirty-nine to forty-four sons. Generally, the proportion of firstborn to the whole male population is one to four.[85]

Keil and Delitzsch handle this problem by arguing that this number of firstborn only represents the number born in the space of thirteen months (or between the exodus and the time when the law was given).[86] This would seem to indicate, on the basis of the above statistics, that there were about 19,000 firstborn in one year, and thus bring the numbers in conformity with the probabilities of the historical situation.

Burials in the wilderness. A problem not usually raised by liberal scholars, but one which is of importance because of its archaeological implications, concerns the death of the whole generation that was first numbered. If over two million people died in a period of 38 to 40 years in a limited amount of territory,

---

[84]*Ibid.,* p. 216.
[85]See Keil and Delitzsch, *loc. cit.*
[86]*Op. cit.,* p. 12.

where are the bodies or their remains? Surely, under normal circumstances, there would be some evidence of mass burials somewhere in the wilderness.

The first step toward the solution of the problem is to examine all the verses that pertain to the deaths of these people in the wilderness. A careful consideration of this data will reveal that with the exception of Moses (Deut. 34:6), Miriam (Num. 20:1), Aaron (Deut. 10:6), and those who died of a plague because of disobedience (Num. 11:34), there is no mention of burials in connection with the deaths in the wilderness. In many texts which describe the reason and causes of death among the first generation, one gets the impression that most, if not all, deaths were the result of immediate, divine judgment (cf. Deut. 2:14, 15; Num. 14:29, 32, 35; Josh. 5:6; I Cor. 10:5, and Jude 5). It appears, that for the most part, burials were carried out on a very limited basis. Apparently most died in such a manner that burial was unnecessary or perhaps there was no one present at the time of death to bury the dead (assuming that the judgment of God completely annihilated the whole population of a given area). In any event, the problem is an interesting one but one which at present cannot be solved with any finality.[87]

Military statistics and census lists. The Old Testament contains abundant records of military operations and these contain rather detailed accounts of the number of men who participated, those who were slain or taken captive, the number of chariots deployed, and even the number of animals slain or taken as booty. Most of the material recorded is beyond question as to its historical validity; however, there are several accounts which have been given considerable attention because of the high numbers recorded.

The most discussed problem of this nature, beside the census lists for the exodus, is the size of David's army as recorded in II Samuel 24:9. According to David's census his military potential consisted of 800,000 men in Israel and 500,000 men in Judah. This would give him a national military potential of some 1,300,000 men. According to the parallel account in I Chronicles

---

[87]A similar problem exists with regard to burials in the area of Goshen.

21:5 the number was even higher (1,570,000 men). The following chart will illustrate the problem at hand:

	II Sam. 24	I Chron. 21	Difference
Israel	800,000	1,100,000	+300,000
Judah	500,000	470,000	− 30,000

Two specific problems are presented by this data: one relates to the differences in the figures between the two accounts, and the other relates to the size of the figures in the two accounts. Most liberal-critical scholars reject these numbers as being both meaningless and unreliable.[88] Since this is the case, little effort is taken to reconcile the figures or to relate them to a historical context.

If the Chronicles record showed increases for both Israel and Judah, it might be argued that the census in II Samuel was incomplete. But such is not the case as the above chart has shown.

Keil and Delitzsch explain the differences between the two lists on the basis of oral tradition:

> The numbers are not given by thousands, and therefore are only approximative statements in round numbers; and the difference in the two texts rose chiefly from the fact, that the statements were merely founded upon oral tradition, since, according to I Chron. 27:4, the result of the census was not inserted in the annals of the kingdom.[89]

Another possible explanation for the differences might be that the lists represent different stages of counting. Perhaps the Samuel account represents completed totals for Judah but not for Israel, while the Chronicles account may be the completed totals for Israel but not for Judah (assuming the larger numbers to be the final totals). The fact that neither of the summaries was placed in the official records of the kingdom (I Chron.

---

[88]Henry P. Smith, *A Critical and Exegetical Commentary on the Books of Samuel; The International Critical Commentary* (New York: Charles Scribner's Sons, 1909), p. 389.

[89]*Biblical Commentary on the Books of Samuel* (Grand Rapids: Wm. B. Eerdmans Publishing Co., 1950), p. 505.

27:24) might be an indication of their incomplete character.

The other problem raised by the figures in these census lists is that of their large size. The problem is explained by DeVaux in the following manner:

> The lower total, in II Samuel, is still far too high: 1,300,000 men of military age would imply at least five million inhabitants, which, for Palestine, would mean nearly twice as many people to the square mile as in the most thickly populated countries of modern Europe. . . . We must simply acknowledge that these figures are artificial.[90]

If David numbered his men in the same manner as Moses (i.e., 20 years and upward), it would mean that the population of Palestine would have to be at least five million or more. This seems like a rather large number for what might appear to be a relatively small area of land. It has been estimated, however, that the boundaries given in II Samuel 24:2-12, with the exception of the Phoenician coast, would include an area of some 12,500 square miles.[91] This being the case, there would be about 310 people per square mile which is not an unreasonable figure.[92]

DeVaux does admit that the census includes a large amount of territory, but still refuses to admit the possibility of that many people occupying it.[93] His statistical arguments appear somewhat vague and general. What he considers the density of population per square mile to be according to II Samuel 24 he does not say, nor does he say what countries of Europe he has in mind. Such arguments, lacking specificity, must be brought under immediate suspicion.

We are not told in the Biblical text just how a military census was taken in ancient times. Perhaps this was carried out by having clan or village leaders conduct a count in their area and then the figures would be turned over to the tribal heads. Tribal chiefs would in turn calculate the statistics for their tribes

---

[90]Op. cit., p. 65.
[91]Keil and Delitzsch, op. cit., p. 7.
[92]Supra, p. 64.
[93]Loc. cit.

and these would then be turned over to a superior, and so on. Herodotus (*Historia,* Book VII) records an interesting account of the method Xerxes used to count his army on one occasion.

> The territory of Doriscus is in Thrace, a wide plain by the sea, and through it flows a great river, the Hebrus; here was built that royal fortress which is called Doriscus, and a Persian guard was posted there by Darius even since the time of his march against Scythia. It seemed, therefore, to Xerxes to be a fit place to array and number his host, and this he did. All the fleet, having now arrived at Doriscus, was brought at his command to neighboring beach . . . and hauled up for rest. . . . In the meanwhile Xerxes numbered his army. . . .

> What the number of each part was I cannot with exactness say, for there is no one who tells us that; but the count of the whole land army showed it to be a million and seven hundred thousand.[94] The numbering was done as follows: a myriad men were collected in one place, and when they were packed together as closely as might be, a line was drawn around them; this being done, the myriad was sent away and a wall of stone built on the line reaching up to a man's navel which done, others were brought into the walled space, till in this way all were counted.[95]

There may be a parallel to this method of counting in II Samuel 8:2 (A.S.V.):

> And he [David] smote Moab and measured them with the line, making them to lie down on the ground; and he measured two lines to put to death, and the one full line to keep alive. And the Moabites became servants to David and brought tribute.[96]

Whatever method was used to number for military purposes, it is apparent that only round numbers were used to record the results.

---

[94]If this total is reliable, we might have a historical parallel to the size of David's army.

[95]Quoted in Tobias Dantzig, *Number the Language of Science* (New York: The Macmillan Company, 1959), pp. 254, 255.

[96]Brackets mine.

To those who would charge that an army of 1,300,000 would be impossible to mobilize in the land of Palestine, we should like to point out that such a vast army was never mobilized. I Chronicles 27:1-15 indicates that the mobilized army of David numbered only 288,000. The purpose of this census in II Samuel 24, as well as the two recorded during the forty years in the wilderness, was to ascertain the national military potential of Israel. The total of men capable of military service must be regarded only as a potential fighting force, for it is unlikely that David or any other Israelite king could fully equip and mobilize a million men or more.

Another text which has been the object of considerable attention is that of I Samuel 15:4. In this account Saul summoned over 200,000 troops to fight the Amalekites. It would appear that this was a rather large army to be used against what seems to be a small and inconsequential nation. But it should be remembered that it was God's command to completely destroy this nation (I Sam. 15:2, 9, 20) and such a command could only be carried out with sufficient forces. It has also been observed that:

> These numbers are not too large; for a powerful Bedouin nation such as the Amalekites were, could not possibly be successfully attacked with a small army, but only by raising the whole of the military force of Israel.[97]

Furthermore, according to I Samuel 15:4, the battle was to be fought in or near Telaim which is generally identified with Telem (Josh. 15:24) in the Negev. This being the case, there would have been sufficient area for an army of that size to mobilize and maneuver. Unfortunately, Saul did not carry out the orders as God commanded (15:9 ff.).

Other texts which have been subject to critical scrutiny because of their large military statistics are Judges 3:31 (600 Philistines slain by Shamgar).[98] Judges 15:15 (Samson's slaying

---

[97]Keil and Delitzsch, *op. cit.*, p. 151.

[98]This is probably a total for his military career involving a number of conflicts.

of 1000 Philistines),[99] I Samuel 11:8 (Saul numbered the fighting men of Israel as 300,000 and the men of Judah as 30,000), and II Kings 19:35 (185,100 Assyrians smitten). These texts have been discussed in the standard commentaries and the principles established above are sufficient to warrant acceptance of these numbers.

One problem related to military statistics which is somewhat unique is that raised in the number of Philistine chariots at Michmash (I Sam. 13:5). The text indicates that the Philistines gathered to fight with Israel and brought with them 30,000 chariots. This appears to be an impossible figure for two reasons: (1) the town of Michmash was located in the hill country of central Palestine which would render a large number of chariots useless, (2) the number is many times in excess of other records of chariot divisions in a single encounter. Pharaoh, for example, only had 600 chariots in pursuit of the Israelites in Exodus 14:7, Sisera 900 (Judg. 4:13) and Zera the Ethiopian 300 (II Chron. 14:8). In the great battle of Qarqar (853 B.C.) the coalition that fought Shalmaneser III only had about 4,000 chariots.[100] The number 30,000 is reduced in the Lucian edition of the LXX text and the Syriac to 3,000, but even this figure is rather large considering the topographical conditions of that area. The answer to the problem might be found in a textual corruption. It has been suggested that the number 1000 is also a possible reading. According to Keil and Delitzsch if this number is the true reading:

> . . . the origin of the number thirty must be attributed to the fact, that through the oversight of a copyist the *lamed* of the word *yiśrā'ēl* was written twice, and consequently the second *lamed* was taken for the numeral thirty.[101]

---

[99]The problem here is most likely one of accepting the miraculous rather than the credibility of the number.

[100]*ANET*, "The Siege of Jerusalem," trans. by A. Leo Oppenheim, pp. 278, 279.

[101]*Op. cit.*, p. 127. This solution, however, assumes too early a use of the alphabet for numerical purposes and therefore is not completely satisfactory.

If 30,000 were reduced to 3000 or 1000 the situation would be historically possible if the chariots were located in the area of Beth-aven (vs. 5) and the troops at Michmash.

There are some indications in extra-Biblical sources that armies and cities, in ancient times, were considerably larger than was previously imagined. Sennacherib, for example, records that he drove out 200,150 people from forty-six cities in Judah.[102] The size of mobilized armies on extended marches accords well with the Biblical records. Joshua, for example used 35,000 in the defeat of Ai (Josh. 8), the Benjamite army numbered 26,000 plus 700 of Gibeah (Judg. 20:15), and the Aramaean army of Zobah was numbered at 20,000 footman (II Sam. 10:6). In II Samuel 17:1 Ahithophel requested 12,000 men to pursue David and his men, and in the fifth year of Rehoboam, Shishak invaded Judah with 60,000 men (II Chron. 12:3). These figures are to be compared with the records of Shalmanezer III who records that Ahab alone contributed 10,000 footman and 2,000 chariots to the coalition army.[103] The estimated size of the coalition army as a whole is 75,000 to 80,000 men.[104] The levy of Shalmanezer III for that battle is reported at about 102,000.[105] In the fourteenth year of his reign he mobilized 120,000 men and crossed the Euphrates at flood season.[106] Mari texts also reveal numbers which are similar in size to Joshua's armies. Mendenhall writes:

> In ARM, I 42, the kingdom of Mari raises a total of 4,000 troops, while Shamsi-Adad of Assyria raises 10,000 and the kingdom of Eshnunna also levies 6,000. The total army numbers 20,000 which may be compared with the army of 22,000 men put in the field by Damascus against King David.[107]

It will be noted that for the most part mobilized armies on extended marches generally range anywhere from 6,000 to 100,000. Let it be emphasized that the figures in extra-Biblical

---

[102]*ANET*, "The Siege of Jerusalem," p. 288.
[103]*Ibid.*, "Texts of Shalmanezer III," p. 279.
[104]Smith, *op. cit.*, p. 2158.
[105]*Ibid.*
[106]*ANET*, "Texts of Shalmanezer III," p. 280.
[107]*Op. cit.*, p. 64.

documents represent a mobilized unit which engaged in a specific encounter. These figures are not to be taken as representing the national potential of any given nation. When this is kept in view, it is apparent that the numbers given in the Bible for the size of armies are within the framework of contemporary history. The census lists of the Old Testament do not represent a mobilized, equipped army and therefore, should not be criticised because of their largeness. One more thing might be added at this point and that is, that one should expect the Israelite armies to have been larger to some extent than perhaps a specified Assyrian or Egyptian army because most of Israel's battles were fought within or near her borders. If Israel had adopted the imperial policies of other nations, and conducted extended campaigns into other lands, we would probably see some reduction in numbers.

Textual Problems

Textual problems relating to numbers usually fall into two classes: (1) problems of omission and (2) problems related to transmission, in which numbers have been changed or added on. It will not be possible to examine all problems in this category, but the more difficult ones will be treated in order to show that such difficulties are not without solution.[108]

Problems involving omissions. One of the clearest examples of the problem of the omission of numbers is I Samuel 13:1. The Hebrew text reads as follows: *Ben šānāh šā'ûl bemālko ušetê šanîm mālak 'al yiśrā'ēl.* A literal translation of this verse would be "The son of (one) year was Saul when he began to reign and he reigned two years over Israel." It is obvious that both statements of this verse are impossible. First, he could not (and did not) reign when he was only one year old. In the second place, it is impossible to fit all the events of Saul's reign into two years. In the light of these problems, most commentators are agreed that the present form of the text suffers

---

[108]Further discussion of these and similar problems may be found in J. W. Wenham, "Large Numbers in the Old Testament," *Tyndale Bulletin* (London: Tyndale Press, 1967), p. 21 f.

from an omission of numbers which were orginally there. The verse apparently contains two omissions and should read as follows: "Saul was ___ years old when he began to reign, and he ruled _____ and two years over Israel."[109] Some attempts have been made to supply the numerical data but these must be viewed with suspicion because of the lack of other statistical data with reference to Saul's period of rule. When such omissions occur, it is generally difficult to replace the missing number and the interpreter is sometimes left with a fragmented verse. One interesting sidelight, however, with reference to the Samuel text quoted above, is the fact that the scribes faithfully copied this verse even though it contained an obvious error.

Problems caused in transmission — The punishment of the men of Beth-shemesh (I Sam. 6:19) is probably one of the outstanding examples of an error in the transmission of numbers. According to the Hebrew text of I Samuel 6:19, Jehovah smote of the people "seventy men, fifty-thousand men" of Beth-shemesh. According to Matthew Pool, who wrote on the problem some years ago, there are three possible meanings which may be assigned to the clause under question.

1. "and he smote of the people seventy men (who had the value of) fifty thousand men."

2. "and he smote of the people seventy men (out of) fifty thousand men."

3. "and he smote of the people seventy men, fifty (out of) a thousand men."[110]

The problem that this verse introduces regards the possibility of that many people living in Beth-shemesh or even being at that place at one time. The above renderings represent some early attempts to solve the problem, although the second suggestion does not help the difficulty of the large population.

It is very doubtful that the expression "fifty thousand" belongs in the text. In the first place, the syntax is irregular in that

---

[109]On this problem see Josephus who states that Saul reigned for twenty years (*Ant.* 10:8:4 and 6:14:9).

[110]*Synopsis* (London, 1669-74), quoted by O. T. Allis, "The Punishment of the Men of Bethshemesh," *The Evangelical Quarterly,* Vol. 15 (Oct. 1943), p. 303.

there is an absence of the conjunction between the first and
second numbers. Another syntactical irregularity exists in the
fact that the small number comes first. In the second place,
there are three Hebrew MSS which omit the number.[111] Thirdly, Josephus claims that seventy died, and does not mention the
"fifty thousand" (*Ant.* 6:1:4). Most commentators feel that the
text has suffered from a gloss.[112]

There have been some attempts, however, to allow the number "fifty-thousand" to remain even though large. One argument is that the plague which smote the inhabitants of Beth-
shemesh had reached them by infection from Philistines; that
it killed first seventy inhabitants of Beth-shemesh and then,
spreading through the countryside, fifty-thousand of the rest of
the people.[113] This view, of course, is purely speculative and
without Biblical support. A more recent attempt to interpret
the verse, leaving the large number to stand, is that of Oswald
T. Allis. He renders the whole clause as follows: "and he smote
of the people seventy men — fifty thousandths of the population."[114] Allis argues that the omission was conjunctive and
can be attributed to a scribal error.[115] He relies heavily on the
fact that the LXX includes the conjunction and also argues that
a *mem* has been lost in the Hebrew text before *'elep*. Since
the word "fifty," which immediately precedes *'elep* ends with a
mem, he feels that a scribe omitted a second *mem* which was
in juxtaposition with *'elep*. He considers that the expression following "seventy men" is an explanatory statement to the effect
that the punishment was on the basis of fifty per thousand. This
view has in its favor at least limited grammatical support, but it

---

[111]Cod, Kenn, 84, 210, 418. See Lange and Schaff, *op. cit., Samuel* p.
116.
[112]C. F. Keil and F. Delitzsch, *Biblical Commentary on the Books of
Samuel,* trans. James Martin (Grand Rapids: Wm. B. Eerdmans Publishing
Co. 1950), p. 68.
    S. R. Driver, *Notes on the Hebrew Text and the Topography of the
Books of Samuel* (Oxford: The Clarendon Press, 1913), p. 58.
[113]See S. Goldman, "Samuel," *The Soncino Books of the Bible,* ed., A.
Cohen (London: The Soncino Press, 1951), p. 34.
[114]*Op. cit.,* p. 306.
[115]An example of this phenomenon can be seen in Neh. 7:12 where the
conjunctive is omitted but in the parallel passage (Ezra 2:39) it is present.

must be apparent that arithmetically the idiom has no parallel and seems to ascribe more mathematical sophistication to the text than it warrants. It is the view of this writer, therefore, that the expression "fifty-thousand" should be regarded as a gloss and be omitted from the text.

There are a number of textual problems that are clearly copyist errors. When contradictory numbers occur in parallel passages, the interpreter must take into view the intent of the passage and the nature of the events, in order to arrive at a conclusion as to which of the two numbers represents the true reading of the text. An example of this phenomenon is found in II Samuel 24:13 where the reading is "seven years" while in the parallel passage the reading is "three years" (I Chron. 21:12). Commentators are generally agreed that the Chronicles passage is probably the better reading:

> Instead of "seven" years of famine Chron. (so Sept.) has "three," agreeing with the figures in the other plagues. For this reason the reading of Chron. is to be preferred. . . .[116]

König argues that the answer to the problem lies in the confusion of letters in the alphabetic system of numeral notation:

> When, for instance, we read in II Sam. 24:13 "seven years," but in the parallel passage I Chron. 21:12 "three years," it is natural to suppose that a confusion has taken place between zayin and gimel.[117]

This solution must be rejected, however, on the grounds that it has not yet been established that the alphabetic system of notation was ever used in the Old Testament. In this case (and ones similar to it) the context of the passage must determine the correct reading.[118]

---

[116]Lange and Schaff, "Samuel," Commentary on the Holy Scriptures, Trans. Philip Schaff (Grand Rapids: Zondervan Publishing Co., n.d.), p. 606.

[117]Op. cit., p. 562.

[118]Similar textual variants are found in II Sam. 8:4; 10:18; I Chron. 18:4; 19:18. Cf. Josephus, Ant. 7:6:3. All these are the results of copyists error according to D. R. Ap-Thomas, "A Numerical Poser," Journal of Near Eastern Studies, Vol. 2 (July, 1943), p. 199. In the New Testament there is confusion of 76 and 276 in the MSS of Acts 27:37 and of 616 and 666 in those of Rev. 13:18.

Some problems of this type can be solved with the aid of the LXX, the versions, and the Dead Sea Scrolls. In Exodus 1:5 (cf. Deut. 10:22; Gen. 46:27) the Masoretic text says that Jacob's descendants numbered seventy when he went to Egypt[119] but the number given in Stephen's speech in Acts 7:14 is seventy-five. The LXX reads seventy-five and it would appear that Stephen was using that translation on that occasion. The question has been, which is correct? A number of attempts have been made to show that Stephen's reckoning was perhaps more inclusive than that of Exodus 1:5 and that essentially both figures are correct.[120] These explanations have been given because there has been a general suspicion about the credibility of the numbers found in the LXX. With the discovery of the Dead Sea Scrolls some scholars are now changing their opinion as to the value of the numbers found in the LXX. In the example cited above the number seventy-five now appears in a Qumran manuscript[121] and seems to support the LXX reading and the quotation of Stephen.

C. Summary

The basic functions of conventional numbers in Scripture involve mathematical processes, specific denotation of quantities or totals, and rounded numbers both small and large which represent literal quantities in estimated form. The most perplexing and difficult problems in the Old Testament are with the conventional (historical) use of large numbers. It was shown that in most cases large numbers should be regarded as reliable

---

[119]See also Josepus in *Ant.* 2:7:4 and 6:5:6.

[120]Henry Alford, *The Greek Testament* (Chicago: Moody Press, rev. ed. 1958), Vol. II, p. 71.

R. C. H. Lenski, *The Interpretation of the Acts of the Apostles* (Columbus, Ohio: The Wartburg Press, 1944), p. 270.

[121]See Millar Burrows, *More Light on the Dead Sea Scrolls* (New York: The Viking Press, 1958), p. 135.

It should be observed, however, that the number seventy does remain in the Qumran texts of Deut. 10:22. See M. Baillet, J. T. Milik, and R. DeVaux, *Discoveries in the Judean Desert of Jordan* III, texts (Oxford: The Clarendon Press, 1962), Fig. 11, Le Phylactere: Groupe IV, p. 155 and Mezouza (Grotte 8), p. 59, line 12.

unless the very possibility of such numbers can be conclusively dismissed. In most cases the context provides sufficient data to demonstrate the reality of such numbers. Liberal critics, who *a priori* dismiss the possibility of Divine intervention supernaturally into the affairs of men, will not, of course, accept these numbers at face value. Textual problems raised by a conflict in parallel accounts can be solved by ascertaining the precise nature of that conflict. Sometimes problems arise from the omission of certain numbers, other times the addition or change of a certain number will be the cause of the difficulty.

On the whole, however, the Bible displays a remarkable degree of exactness in its employment of numbers and this, it may be added, in an age when such arithmetical exactness was not common.

Chapter 4

THE RHETORICAL USE OF NUMBERS

A very important use of numbers in the Old Testament is that for rhetorical or poetic effect. Whenever numbers are so used, they are not to be understood literally nor symbolically. Much effort has been expended attempting to ascertain some hidden or mysterious meaning of rhetorical phrases using numbers. The intention of the writer in this usage is not to emphasize the mathematical value of the number primarily, but to express either intensity or other concepts such as "few," "many," etc.

There are, therefore, two basic applications of numbers in poetic structure.

A. The Climactic Use of Numbers

The arrangement of a numeral with its sequel within a clause, either syndetically or asyndetically, in Scripture is a common poetic device with numerous parallels in contemporary literature. The intention of such a device is to express the concept of intensification and/or progression. The actual value of the numbers in such cases is not significant.

This phenomenon is perhaps best expressed in the formula $x/x+1$.[1] It occurs principally in poetic passages but not exclusively. Syntactically $x/x+1$ may appear in the same sentence or in two different sentences. In most instances in the Old Testament it appears in poetical passages employing synonomous, synthetic and antithetical parallelisms. The following is a list of the occurrences of the $x/x+1$ sequences in the Old Testament:

Sequence 1/2 — Judges 5:30; Deuteronomy 32:30; II Kings 6:10; Jeremiah 3:14; Psalm 62:11; Job 33:14; 40:5; Ezra 10:13; Nehemiah 13:20.

---

[1]This formula is adopted from W. M. W. Roth, "The Numerical Sequence $x/x+1$ in the Old Testament," *Vetus Testamentum*, XII (July 1962).

Sequence 2/3 — Deuteronomy 17:6; II Kings 9:32; Isaiah 17:6; Hosea 6:2; Amos 4:8; Job 33:29.

Sequence 3/4 — Exodus 20:5; 34:7; Numbers 14:8; Deuteronomy 5:9; Jeremiah 36:23; Amos 1:3, 6, 9, 11, 13; 2:1, 4, 6; Proverbs 30:15, 18, 21, 29.

Sequence 4/5 — Isaiah 17:6

Sequence 5/6 — II Kings 13:19

Sequence 6/7 — Job 5:19; Proverbs 6:16

Sequence 7/8 — Micah 5:4

Sequence 8/9 — none.

Sequence 9/10 — none.

Sequence 1000/10,000 — Deuteronomy 32:30; I Samuel 18:7; 21:11; 29:5; Psalm 91:7.

The above list includes occurrences of this type of expression in both prose and poetic passages and it does not distinguish between the two fundamental types of occurrence.[2]

X/x+1 As a Poetic Device

The most striking use of this device is found in poetic portions of the Old Testament. It is frequently employed in synonymous, synthetic and antithetic parallelisms and when it is thus employed, the numbers should generally be regarded as parallel. Roth explains this point in the following manner:

> Since there is no other expression for a given numeral than the numeral itself, the numeral one unit lower serves as a parallel term; a phenomenon as strange to us as it is characteristic of Semitic poetic parallelism.[3]

In this usage of x/x+1 formula there is little or no regard for the actual mathematical value of the numbers employed. For example, Amos speaks of the anger of Yahweh in the following manner:

> . . . for three transgressions of Damascus, yea, for four, I will not turn away the punishment thereof. . . .[4]

---

[2]One type is when the expression x/x+1 occurs in one sentence and the other is when it occurs in two separate sentences.

[3]*Op. cit.*, p. 304.

[4]Amos 1:3; cf. 1:6, 9, 11, 13; 2:1, 4, 6.

It is evident that the writer is not attempting to total the sins of Damascus, Tyre, Gaza, etc., for the sins enumerated are in most cases neither three nor four. The purpose is to show climax and finality by means of numbers in progression. In fact, the fundamental function of this idiom is to strengthen and intensify the parallelism in such a manner that the reader cannot escape its impact. This observation is clearly illustrated in the following examples where the wrath or the end of patience is the theme:

> For God speaketh once, yea twice, though man regardeth it not (Job. 33:14 ASV).

> Once have I spoken, and I will not answer; Yea, twice but I will proceed no further. (Job 40:5 ASV).

Micah also illustrates this phenomenon:

> . . . then shall we raise against him seven shepherds, and eight principal men (Micah 5:5 ASV).

In each one of the above examples other numbers could have been substituted and the meaning or impact would not have been violated. The precise literary value of the formula $x/x+1$ was not recognized until recent years when contemporary inscriptions were made to bear on Hebrew grammar and syntax. Older grammarians concluded that numbers in this arrangement merely expressed "a number not exactly specified or an indefinite total."[5] This analysis is not incorrect, but merely incomplete. There are cases when juxtaposition of two numbers in progression do indicate an indefinite total, but these do not constitute the majority of cases. With the appearance of Ugaritic poetry, the Biblical student had at his disposal a rich supply of cognate parallels for this numerical phenomenon. This literary device was used freely by the scribes at Ugarit and with considerable effectiveness. In the Baal Epic, the $x/x+1$ sequence of numbers is used to create literary climax with regard to Baal's view of sacrifice:

---

[5] E. Kautzsch, ed., *Gesenius' Hebrew Grammar*, 2nd. ed. rev. by A. E. Cowley (Oxford: The Clarendon Press, 1910), p. 437.

> For two [kinds of] banquets Baal hates,
> Three the rider of the clouds:
> A banquet [banquet] of baseness,
> And a banquet of handmaids' lewdness.
> (Baal II. iii, 16-21).[6]

After Baal was furnished with a temple, he made a journey to claim the domains which were rightly his. The description of the journey employs climactic numbers:

> Sixty-six towns he took,
> Seventy-seven hamlets;
> Eighty [took] Baal of [Zaphon's] s[ummit],
> Ninety Baal of the sum[mit].
> (Baal II. vii, 9-12).[7]

It appears that the scribes utilized this device to intensify the emotion of a given event or act, for in the majority of occurrences of this phenomenon strong emotions (e.g., anger, love, etc.) or violent actions are expressed. In the Baal and 'Anat epics there is a good example of this practice. Baal apparently meets with a tragic death and the weeping, mourning, etc. of the other gods is described in vivid language. In this portion of the text, which is rather fragmented, there are no less than five occurrences of climactic numbers.[8] Note the intense sadness and frustration of this occasion:

> Wine of iš [ryt]
> number [   ]
> Like the seven cries of his mouth
> Yea his eight shrieks.
> The sun —
> She goes to seek [   ]
> The Sun after him [   ]
> One place, two places [   ]
> One place, two places [   ]

6*ANET*, p. 132.

7*Ibid.*, p. 134.

8Cyrus H. Gordon, *Ugaritic Literature* (Roma: Pontificium Institutum Biblicum, 1949), pp. 55, 56.

THE RHETORICAL USE OF NUMBERS   97

> The foundation(s) of the sea [   ]
> Weeping, fills [   ]
> Tears of [   ]⁹

The Legend of Krt,[10] and the Legend of Aght,[11] also contain
numerous examples of climactic numbers. Aramaean literature
also gives evidence of this practice. In an Aramaean Magical
text dating from the seventh century B.C. the following appears:

> [w] ives of Hauron, whose utterance is true and his seven
> concubines and the eight wives of Baal.[12]

Examples of this literary device are not common in Akkadian
literature. When numerical climaxes do occur, they are more
subtle and not as redundant as in the case with Ugaritic epics.
The more common form of this sequence is used in relation with
days and nights.[13] In *Die Assyrische Beschworungssammlung
Maqlu* there are two passages dealing with incantations against
witches which employ numerical climax:

> He, meine Zauberin oder meine Spukmacherin,
> die auf *eine* Meile ein Feuer anzündet,
> auf *zwei* Meilin ihren Boten geschickt hat. . .[14]

> *Zwei* sind die Töchter des Himmelsgottes Anu,/
> *Drei* sind die Töchter des Himmelsgottes Anu.[15]

When an ancient scribe wished to express magnitude along with
intensity of expression in a parallelism he would, in most cases,
employ large numbers for his x/x+1 sequence. A favorite

---

⁹*Ibid.,* p. 56.
¹⁰*Ibid.,* Text 128: II:20, p. 75, Cf. *ANET,* p. 143.
¹¹*Ibid.,* Text 3:30 ff., p. 93.
¹²W. F. Albright, "An Aramaean Magical Text in Hebrew From the
Seventh Century B.C." *Bulletin of the American Schools of Oriental Research,* No. 76 (Dec., 1939), p. 9.
¹³Cf. "The Epic of Gilgamesh," Table VII:iv:10, *ANET,* p. 87.
¹⁴Gerhard Meier, ed., *Die Assyrische Beschworungssammlung Maqlu*
(Berlin, 1937), p. 45 quoted by Roth, *op. cit.,* p. 305 (italics mine).
¹⁵*Ibid.,* (italics mine).

combination of the scribes at Ugarit was 1000/10,000. In a banquet scene recorded in the Baal and Anat cycles the following
passage attempts to show the great amount of the wine presented to Baal:

> He stands, serves liquor, and gives him drink.
> He places a cup in his hand,
> A flagon in the grasp of his hand;
> A vessel large and conspicuous,
> A jar to dumbfound a mortal;
> A holy cup of woman ne'er seen,
> Only Asherah beholds such a flagon.
> He takes a thousand pots of wine,
> Mixes ten thousand in his mixture.[16]

Later in the epic we read:

> [O'er] thousand ["fields" in the] sea.
> Ten thousand [acres] in the floods.
> [Tra]verse Gabel, traverse Qa'al,
> Traverse Ihat-nop-shamem . . .
>
> From a thousand fields, ten thousand acres,
> At Kotha[r]'s feet bow and fall down,
> Prostrate thee and do him honor.[17]

This literary device was also known to the Old Testament
scribes and was used by them on numerous occasions. The
question raised in Deuteronomy 32:30 is an example of this
phenomenon:

> How should one chase a thousand,
> and two put ten thousand to flight,
> except their rock had sold them,
> and the Lord had shut them up?[18]

Again in Psalm 91:7 we read:

> A thousand shall fall at thy side,

---

[16]"Poems about Baal and Anath" (VAB, A,) *ANET,* p. 136.
[17]*Ibid.,* (VAB, F,) *ANET,* p. 138. Cf. also Baal II, viii, 24, p. 135.
[18]*KJV.*

> and ten thousand at thy right hand;
> but it shall not come nigh thee.[19]

The other occurrences of this expression are found in antithetic parallelisms. The song dedicated to David employs these two numbers and their effectiveness is illustrated by Saul's immediate response.[20]

> And the women answered one another
> as they played, and said,
> Saul hath slain his thousands, and[21]
> David his ten thousands (I Sam. 18:7 KJV).

"It is obvious that in this verse the two numbers are contrasted with each other in accordance with the intention of the verse, that is, the exaltation of David over Saul."[22] The interpretation of numbers which occur in the numerical sequence $x/x+1$ in synonymous, synthetic and antithetic parallelisms, therefore, must be interpreted in the light of the literary idiom and context, not necessarily the actual value of the number. This does not mean that the numbers employed in the $x/x+1$ sequence in parallelism never have mathematical value, for they quite commonly do. Their literary and/or mathematical values must be determined by the context alone.

X/x+1 As a Mathematical Expression

As observed above, there are instances when the climactic formula $x/x+1$ does have actual numerical value. When this formula takes on numerical value, it will usually be found in the opening lines of a text, and the value usually referred to will be the second number given (i.e., $x+1$). Proverbs 30:18 reads:

---

[19]*Ibid.*

[20]I Sam. 18:8. This song gained such wide popularity that even the Philistines knew of it (cf. I Sam. 29:5).

[21]The translation of the conjunction here is better "but" than "and" since the poetry is in antithetic parallelism. Cf. also I Sam. 21:11.

[22]Roth, *op. cit.*, p. 303.

> There be three things which are too wonderful for me, yea,
> four which I know not.[23]

In the verses that follow four things are actually listed. Ugaritic
literature also employs the x/x+1 sequence in the same manner.
In the Baal Epic, to which we have already alluded,[24] there is
an excellent example of this phenomenon:

> Baal hates two sacrifices,
> Three, the Rider of Clouds:
> The sacrifice of shame
> And the sacrifice of baseness
> And the sacrifice of the murmur of handmaids.[25]

Examples of numerical sayings of this type are also found in
Aramaic. In the Ahiqar text from Elephantine, which is probably of Mesopotamian origin, the following has been preserved:

> Two things are an ornament (to a man),
> of three there is pleasure to šamaš:
> One who drinks [?] wine
> and also gives it [to others] to drink,
> one who restrains [his] wisdom . . . [?]
> and [one who] hears a thing and does not reveal [it to others].[26]

In the above examples the literary force of the numerical
phrase is the same as the examples cited in synonymous parallelisms, but with the additional factor of the numbers having actual mathematical values. In all cases examined, in both the
Bible and extra-Biblical literature, the only number receiving
literal values was the second (x+1) which was always the higher
number.

B.   The Idiomatic Use of Numbers

X/x+1 as an indefinite value. In the Old Testament and in
extra-Biblical literature there is a large group of numerical sayings that are, in meaning, different from the above, but at the

---

[23]*KJV* cf. Ps. 62:11; Job 5:19; 33:14; 40:5; Prov. 6:16; 30:15, 21, 29.
[24]*Supra*, p. 96.
[25]Cyrus H. Gordon, *op. cit.*, p. 30.
[26]A. Cowley, *op. cit.*, p. 215 (col. IV, 92-93a).

same time share in some fundamental structual similarities. In both poetical and prose portions of the Old Testament there are numerous times when the sequence x/x+1 is found as one phrase in one sentence. The numbers either appear asyndetically one beside the other or are joined by the waw conjunction, especially when a preposition or negation stands between the two numbers.[27] The following Old Testament passages belong to this group:

> . . . a *maiden* or *two* for every man (Judg. 5:30) . . . who is on my side? Who? *Two* or *three* eunuchs looked out at him (II Kings 9:32) . . . we cannot stand in the open. Nor is this a work for *one* day or for *two* . . . (Ezra 10:13).

> On the evidence of *two* witnesses or of *three* witnesses he that is to die shall be put to death . . . (Deut. 17:6).

> Gleanings will be left in it, as when an olive tree is beaten — *two* or *three* berries in the top of the highest bough, *four* or *five* on the branches of a fruit tree . . . (Isa. 17:6).

> So *two* or *three* cities wandered to one city . . . (Amos 4:8).[28]

The same sequence is employed in the New Testament:

> For where *two* or *three* are gathered together in my name, there am I in the midst of them (Matt. 18:20).

> Now there were six waterpots of stone set there after the Jews' manner of purifying, containing *two* or *three* firkins apiece (John 2:6).[29]

In all these instances the addition of the second number calls attention to the fact that the first number is not meant to be an exact sum. When, therefore, the sequence x/x+1 appears in juxtaposition in a single phrase, the reference is always to a somewhat indefinite numerical value. Perhaps it is intended to express the concept of a "few" or "a small number."

There are abundant parallels to this phenomenon in extra-

---

[27]Cf. Roth, *op. cit.*, p. 308.
[28]All verses from *RSV*. Cf. also Jer. 3:14; Job 33:29; Exod. 20:5; II Kings 13:9; Eccles. 11:2; and Jer. 36:23.
[29]ASV. Also cf. I Cor. 14:29 (italics mine).

Biblical texts. In the Gilgamesh Epic (Old Babylonian Version),
Tablet II, col. II, lines 6, 7, the following sequence occurs:

> For six days and seven nights Enkidu
> came forth
> Mating with the 1 [ass].[30]

The Middle Assyrian Laws also provide a parallel:

> If a seignior's wife, having deserted her husband, has entered
> the house of an Assyrian, whether it was in the same city or
> in some neighboring city, where he set her up in a house,
> [and] she stayed with the mistress of the house [and] spent
> the night [there] *three* [or] *four* times, without the master of
> the house knowing that the seignior's wife was staying in his
> house . . .[31]

Evidence for the use of this literary device in Egyptian and
Hittite cultures is found in the two versions of the "Treaty Between the Hittites and Egypt."

> . . . if a man or two men — no matter who flee . . . (Egyptian
> version).

In all instances the sequence x/x+1 has the idea of a "few."

C. Summary

In the Old Testament and in contemporary Semitic and non-
Semitic inscriptions the numerical sequence x/x+1 can be utilized
in two ways: (1) It may be employed in a synonymous, synthetic or antithetic parallelism and when it is so employed, it
functions to climax or intensify the sense. The numbers may or
may not have mathematical values. The determination of possible numerical values in this usage must be derived from the
context in which the expression occurs. (2) It could be
used merely to indicate a concept such as a "few." In most instances of this type the sequence occurs in the same phrase and
it may or may not take the conjunction.

---

[30]Translated by E. A. Speiser, *ANET*, p. 77.

[31]Law No. 24, Translator Theophile J. Meek, *ANET*, p. 182 (italics
mine).

[32]Egyptian version translated by John A. Wilson, *ANET*, p. 200.
Hittite version translated by Albrecht Goetze, *ANET*, p. 203.

Chapter 5

THE SYMBOLIC USE OF NUMBERS

Biblical symbolism is, in many respects, one of the most difficult subjects with which one must deal in the science of hermeneutics. The idea of symbolic numbers raises several questions which are unique to this subject, and present the interpreter with what appears to be an insurmountable difficulty. The first question which must be discussed regards the actual existence of symbolic numbers in the Bible. To most interpreters, this might seem like a settled question, but there is by no means unanimous opinion concerning the reality of symbolic numbers in the Bible. Casper Levias, for example, declares that:

> In the Bible itself there is no reference to numerical gematria, or the symbolic use of numbers, and their existence can not be positively demonstrated.[1]

The same writer further argues that ". . . a distinct connection between any given number and a certain idea cannot be proved."[2] Oswald T. Allis maintains a position which is similar to that of Levias:

> The only number in Scripture which is declared to be symbolic is "666" which is the number of the beast (Rev. 13:18).[3]

On the other hand, most scholars see in Scripture a consistent use of numbers which seem to bear a significance over and above their normal arithmetical values.

> The frequency of certain numbers in connection with cultic concerns suggests that these numbers had special significance and importance of themselves, or as symbols of something

---

[1]"Gematria" *The Jewish Encyclopedia,* Isidore Singer, ed. (New York: Funk and Wagnals, 1905), V, p. 589.

[2]"Numbers and Numerals," *Ibid.,* IX, p. 348.

[3]"Bible Numerics," *Baker's Dictionary of Theology,* ed. Everett F. Harrison (Grand Rapids: Baker Book House, 1960), p. 381.

deemed significant. The reasons for the special importance of some of the sacred numbers are rarely simple or obvious.[4]

The view of M. H. Pope is that of most writers on this subject. There are, however, varying degrees of opinion with regard to which numbers are used symbolically and when they are so used. It is the view of this writer that the Bible does employ numbers in a significant or symbolic sense, but on a very limited basis. Further discussion of this position and the reasons for it will be presented below.[5]

A. The Origin of Symbolic Numbers

One's view on the origin of symbolic numbers will generally depend on the nature and scope of his studies in the Bible. Many writers, such as Ethelbert W. Bullinger,[6] Karl G. Sabiers,[7] R. McCormack,[8] M. Mahan,[9] Ivan Panin,[10] and J. Edwin Hartill,[11] attribute symbolic numbers to the direct revelation of God. They usually take a rather uncritical view of these numbers and their reasoning as to the meaning of such numbers is almost totally subjective. They speak of these symbolic numbers as if the Old Testament writers were the first to use them and when they did, it was generally with mystic implications. Unfortunately this viewpoint is that generally accepted by pastors and popular Bible teachers without question.

There is a larger group of scholars[12] which contends that symbolic or significant numbers were in use before the writing of

---

[4]"Number," *The Interpreters Dictionary of the Bible,* p. 564.

[5]*Infra.,* p. 115 ff.

[6]*Number in Scripture* (London: Eyre and Spottiswoode, 1894).

[7]*Astounding New Discoveries* (Los Angeles: Robertson Publishing Co., 1941).

[8]*Seven in Scripture* (London: Marshall Brothers Limited, 1926).

[9]*Palmoni or the Numerals of Scripture* (New York: D. Appleton and Co., 1863).

[10]"Bible Numerics," *Things to Come* (London: Horace Marshall & Son), Vols. 17, 18 (1911, 1912).

[11]*Biblical Hermeneutics* (Grand Rapids: Zondervan Publishing House, 1947).

[12]And one which is rapidly growing as new extra-Biblical materials come to light.

the Old Testament and were a common literary device of scribes from Babylon, Egypt, etc. Within this group of scholars there is division of opinion as to the specific origin of symbolic numbers. Some attribute their origin to the fact that certain numbers have special or unique factors involved in their coefficients.[13] This view is generally disregarded because it is highly speculative and presupposes mathematical developments in early history which are without historiographical support. Another proposal is that the universe exhibits certain numerological phenomena which had its origin in God. Man, according to this view, was influenced by this numerical phenomena and symbolism of numbers was the result.[14] Caspar Levias proposes a view very similar to this:

> At an early time in the history of man certain numbers were regarded as having sacred significance or were used with symbolical force, the origin of their symbolism lying in their connection with primitive ideas about nature and God.[15]

There are some scholars, primarily mathematicians, who argue that the origin of symbolic numbers should be traced to priestly scribes, mainly in Egypt, who began or aided the development of number systematization.[16] Others, according to Van der Waerden, attribute this development to the common scribe who was not part of the temple or priesthood.[17] There is no doubt that the priests and their scribes played an important role in the development of mathematics. But as to the time and place of the early origin of symbolical numbers, we can only speculate. This procedure is necessary because most of the early texts containing numbers from Babylon, for example, are not mythological or mystical but economic. Neugebauer's observation is significant with regard to this situation:

> . . . for the earliest period of writing the economic records are almost the only class of existing documents and the num-

---

[13]Eduard König, *op. cit.*, p. 566.

[14]*Ibid.*

[15]*Op. cit.*, p. 348.

[16]See Van der Waerden, *Science Awakening* (New York: Oxford University Press, 1961), p. 15.

[17]*Ibid.*, p. 17.

ber signs are among those signs which one can read with cer-
tainty even for periods where the interpretation of the other
signs is very problematic.[18]

It would appear that the early symbolical employment of numbers would have been with the priestly scribes since they had
at their disposal both mathematical abilities as well as religious
interests. The merger of the two would be most natural. In
fact, the man who was skilled in the art of mathematical
calculations was considered as being endowed with almost
supernatural powers.[19] It would be natural for an individual so
regarded to exploit this situation not only economically but
religiously. It would appear, therefore, that from a literary
standpoint, the early development of the system of symbolic
numbers should be attributed to the priestly scribes from Egypt
and Babylonia. This question is beyond the possibility of final
solution in the light of the data with which one must work at
present. The origin of the idea or system of symbolic numbers
might be due to two factors: (1) the original revelations of
God to Scripture writers and/or (2) the observations of the
scribes and writers (both of the Bible and other literature) with
regard to natural phenomena of the universe both structual
and chronological in nature.

B.   The Development of Symbolic Numbers

The Old Testament period (*c. 2000 B.C. — 400 B.C.*). The
earliest appearance of symbolical numbers in any quantity was
during the age of Hammurabi in Babylonia. There appears to
be some use of numbers symbolically prior to this time, but the
evidence for this is meager and many times ambiguous.[20] Some
trace numerical symbolism back to the Sumerians:

---

[18]*The Exact Sciences in Antiquity* (New York: Harper & Brothers, 1952),
p. 18.
[19]Tobias Dantzig, *Number, The Language of Science* (The Macmillan
Co., 1959), p. 25.
[20]Limited number symbolism is in evidence from the age of Gudea.
The number most frequently used was 7. See William T. Smith, "Number,"
op. cit., IV, p. 2159.

>There is clear evidence in the cuneiform texts, which are our earliest authorities, that the Babylonians regarded 7 as the number of totality, of completeness. The Sumerians, from whom the Semitic Babylonians seem to have borrowed the idea, equated 7 and "all."[21]

Since almost all of the early texts employing numbers are economic in nature it is difficult to conclusively support the idea that the Sumerians used numbers symbolically to any extent. There was probably some use of numbers in this manner, but how widespread and how well developed this system was, cannot be determined with present epigraphical materials.[22] During the age of Hammurabi and following, a rather large quantity of literary productions appeared which did employ some numbers in a symbolic manner. In the "Creation Epic" Marduk is given fifty names[23] which according to E. A. Speiser, the translator, are meant to be "cabalistic and symbolic."[24] In the old Babylonian version of "The Epic of Gilgamesh" there seems to be a regular employment of 7 in a symbolic manner.[25] Early Egyptian documents show little, if any, employment of number symbolism. The literature of Ugarit, however, is replete with examples of this phenomenon. The number appearing most frequently is 7 and its multiples (esp. 70).[26] It appears from all the evidence examined that number symbolism was employed on a rather limited basis and it appears that very few numbers were employed in this manner. It was not until the age of Pythagoras (sixth cent. B.C.) that number symbolism received systematic treatment. Pythagoras, a student of Thales, was one of the greatest thinkers of his day. He was a well-traveled

---

[21]*Ibid.*

[22]There are some signs in "Gilgamesh and the Land of the Living" of a preference for the numbers seven and fifty. Whether this is merely a stylistic device for rhetorical purposes or actual number symbolism cannot be determined. Cf. *ANET*, p. 48.

[23]*ANET*, p. 69, line 122.

[24]*Ibid.*, n. 112.

[25]*Ibid.* p. 76, Tablet II:ii:6; Tablet IV:v:46; Tablet VII:iv:10; Tablet XI:77, 147, 218, 228, etc.

[26]Cyrus Gordon, *Ugaritic Literature*, p. 27, "Baal and 'Anat" 130:20; p. 35, 51:VI:45; p. 43, VI:62:15-29; p. 47, 49:V:9; etc.

man having visited Babylon, India and Egypt. He based his philosophy upon the postulate that number was the source of the various qualities of manner and was the basis for meaningful knowledge of the universe. This led him to dwell upon the mystic and symbolic properties of numbers and their relationships. The followers of Pythagoras expanded his ideas and methods until almost every number was given some special value symbolically:

> Strikingly similar to the Babylonian was the number worship of the Pythagoreans. It almost seems as if for fear of offending a number by ignoring it, they attributed divine significance to most numbers up to fifty.[27]

According to the Pythagoreans even numbers were soluble, and therefore ephemeral, feminine, pertaining to the earthly; odd numbers were regarded as indissoluble, masculine, partaking of the celestial nature. Each number was identified with some human attribute. "One" stood for reason because it was unchangeable, "two" represented opinion, "four" symbolized justice because it was the first perfect square, the product of equals, etc.[28] There were, in this system, "perfect" numbers. Consider the number 14 as an example. If one would add up its divisors which are 1, 2 and 7, he would get 10. The number 14 is therefore greater than the sum of its own divisors, and is for this reason called "excessive." On the other hand, the sum of the divisors of 12 is 16. Since the sum of the divisors is more than the number, the number 12 would be regarded as "defective." A "perfect" number was a number in which there was neither an excess nor a deficiency, the number would equal the sum of its own divisors. The numbers 6 and 28, therefore, would be considered "perfect" numbers. This number mysticism was developed in both Greece and Italy under the influence of

---

[27]Tobias Dantzig, *op. cit.*, p. 39.

[28]There is a striking correspondence in Chinese mythology to the Pythagorean system of analysis. Odd numbers were symbolized white, day, heat, sun, fire; the even numbers black, night, cold, matter, water, earth. The numbers were arranged on a holy board, the Lo-Chou, which had magical properties when properly used. See Dantzig, *op. cit.*, pp. 40, 41.

Pythagoras and it then spread into Palestine. The efforts of Pythagoras appear to be the first significant attempt to systematically organize numerological data into thought or concept patterns. While the earlier Babylonians, Aramaeans, and Egyptians may have employed numbers rhetorically and symbolically, it is not clear just how far these numbers were actually associated with specific ideas. It is the view of this writer that the development of number symbolism and mysticism with regard to theological precepts must be traced to Pythagoras and not the writers of the Old Testament. Nowhere in the Old Testament is any number given conceptual value or identified with a specific theological truth. Whatever has been deduced with regard to the significance of symbolic numbers has been on the basis of the association of that number with the subject matter in its context.[29]

The intertestamental period (400 B.C. − 15 B.C.). The intertestamental period was a significant period in the development of symbolic numbers. In fact, the whole pseudo-science of mystic numbers received considerable treatment during this era. The Apocrypha and Pseudepigrapha give evidence of the influence of the Old Testament as well as the number theories of Pythagoras. The Apocalyptic writings employed symbolic numbers with considerable freedom. The numbers 3, 4, 7, 10 and 12 occur with regularlity and appear to be used both rhetorically and symbolically.[30] In the Qumran literature the numbers 7, 70 and 490 are quite common. The Apocrypha generally follows the numerical patterns of the Old Testament. Rhetorically, the $x/x+1$ pattern is quite common;[31] symbolically, there seems to be a preference for the number 7 as in the Old Testament.[32] There appears to be some Pythagorean influence in these writings. Wisdom of Solomon 11:20 reads as follows:

> . . . but thou hast arranged all things by measure and number and weight.

---

[29]More extended treatment of this view is given on p. 119 ff.

[30]D. S. Russel, *The Method and Message of Jewish Apocalyptic* (Philadelphia: The Westminster Press, 1964), p. 127.

[31]Cf. Ecclesiasticus 38:17; 13:7; 23:16; 26:28; 26:5, etc.

[32]Cf. II Esdras 13:1; Ecclesiasticus 7:3; 20:12; 22:12, etc.

The universal arrangement of all things by number was clearly a Pythagorean doctrine and not one found in the Old Testament. The number 70 was not only used openly, but there may be some evidence for a rather subtle use of that number symbolically. In II Esdras the word "secret" occurs many times. The Hebrew word _sod_ (secret) has the value of 70 according to the sum of the numerical value of its letters. It is possible, however, that this occurrence is merely coincidental. The Pseudepigrapha also provides examples of the use of numbers symbolically.[33]

During the intertestamental era, numbers were given considerable attention by teachers interested in future events. Numerical patterns were manipulated quite frequently (and freely) by these teachers in order to predict certain events, and this practice led to considerable frustration on the part of the people. Russel comments:

> . . . in their attempts to fulfil unfulfilled prophecy, they make fairly frequent use of what we might call allegorical arithmetic in which much play is made with figures and cycles and number patterns. Such calculations as these led inevitably to frustration and disappointment on the part of the people when it was found that the appointed time had come and gone and the end was not yet.[34]

The frustrations experienced by these early peoples are experienced today by well-meaning Christian people who uncritically accept the numerical calculations of popular prophetic teachers who have a flair for the spectacular. Apparently "allegorical arithmetic" has an appeal to many peoples under differing cultural and historical circumstances.

The New Testament and post-apostolic era (15 B.C. – 500 A.D.). The New Testament employs numbers in large quantities, but apart from the book of Revelation, it does not tend to use numbers symbolically. The most common number employed in this manner in Revelation is the number 7. This use of 7 is best understood literally with symbolic intentions. For

---

[33]Cf. Enoch 24:1; 76:1; IV Ezra 9:23, 28; 13:1.
[34]_Op. cit._, p. 187.

example, in Revelation 1:4 there is mention of the "seven churches in Asia." There is no doubt as to the literal nature of this number for seven churches did indeed exist in Asia at that time. But the fact that there were more than seven in Asia at that time indicates that the writer is using the number symbolically or ideally. Hieropolis and Colossae were both located in the province of Asia (Col. 1:2; 4:13, 15-16), but are not dealt with in Revelation. Other occurrences of the number 7 in Revelation are as follows: 1:12 (candlesticks), 1:16 (stars), 1:20 (angels), 4:5 (lamps), 1:4; 3:1; 4:5 (spirits), and 5:1 (seals).[35] There are some uses of other numbers used in a special way in the New Testament but these, for the most part, are the result of Old Testament influence. The observations of Hopper on this point are significant:

> To be sure, later New Testament exegeticists were able to discover numerical secrets everywhere in the life and preaching of Jesus, but it is obvious to the most casual reader, that such scholarly interpretation is utterly at variance with the Spirit of naivete and directness which distinguishes the Scriptual accounts. The Pauline epistles . . . are completely innocent of the number theory. The synoptic Gospels, together with . . . John and the Acts . . . do contain numbers, but these are "symbolic" only in the most elementary sense.[36]

Two texts which have been given considerable treatment are Revelation 13:18 (number of the beast, 666) and the 153 fishes of John 21:11. Both of these texts and the interpretations given to them will be discussed in Chapter VI.

Since the New Testament does not reflect an abundant use of symbolic numbers, it makes it a rather unique document for its times. If it were merely the product of human genius, it certainly would have exhibited some use of symbolic and mystic numerology which were so popular in Palestine at that time.

With the rise of the Gnostic heresies in the Apostolic and post-Apostolic era, considerable attention was given to the the-

---

[35]Cf. also 5:6; 8:2; 10:3; 13:1; 15:1, 7; 17:3, 9, 10.

[36]*Medieval Number Symbolism* (New York: Columbia University Press, 1938), p. 69.

ological value of numbers and their mystical use in Scripture. The Gnostics relied rather heavily on mystical numerology in support of their views. The numerological data presented by the Gnostics were indeed impressive and seemed to indicate that divine truth could be expressed and explained with such phenomena. In the light of this vast corpus of numerological data Irenaeus raised the following question:

> Is it a meaningless and accidental thing, that the positions of names, and the election of the apostles, and the working of the Lord, and the arrangement of created things, are what they are?[37]

Irenaeus answered his question in the negative, but quickly pointed out that no one should:

> . . . seek to prosecute inquiries respecting God by means of numbers, syllables, and letters. For this is an uncertain mode of proceeding, on account of their varied and diverse systems, and because every sort of hypothesis may at the present day be, in like manner, devised by any one; so that they can derive arguments against the truth from these very theories, insomuch as they may be turned in many different directions.[38]

It would appear from this quotation that Irenaeus was a rather severe critic of the whole system of mystical numerology, but such is clearly not the case. In other places he appears to criticize the conclusions of the Gnostics, but does not demand that their numbers or numerological analysis is a fallacious thing in itself. In *Against Heresies*, he takes the Gnostics to task for their perverse use of the number 5 to establish certain doctrines. His polemic is as follows:

> Any one, in fact, might collect many thousand other things of the same kind, both with respect to this number and any other he chose to fix upon, either from the Scriptures, or from the works of nature lying under his observation. But although

---

[37]*Against Heresies*, Book II:25:1, *The Ante-Nicene Fathers*, Alexander Roberts and James Donaldson, eds., (Grand Rapids: Wm. B. Eerdmans Publishing Co., 1951), Vol. 1, p. 396.

[38]*Ibid.*

such is the case, we do not therefore affirm that there are five Aeons above the Demiurge; nor do we consecrate the Pentad, as if it were some divine thing; nor do we strive to establish things untenable, nor ravings such as they indulge in by means of that vain kind of labour; nor do we perversely force a creation well adapted by God for the ends intended to be served, to change itself into types of things which have no real existence; nor do we seek to bring forward impious and abominable doctrines, the detection and overthrow of which are easy to all possessed of intelligence.[39]

Irenaeus, of all the Fathers, was perhaps the most severe critic of the numerological speculations of the Gnostics. The other Fathers, however, recognized the theological errors of the Gnostic heresies, but seemed to feel that theological propositions or truths could be supported by numerological data. Justin Martyr, for example, supported his argument for monotheism by quoting Pythagoras.[40] Following the lead of Philo and finding justification in the apparent meaninglessness of literal interpretation of certain Scriptural passages, some of the Church Fathers began to write figurative interpretations of Biblical texts. They found precedent for giving importance to numbers in the precise directions given for the dimensions of the tabernacle[41] and in the Wisdom of Solomon which states that ". . . God has arranged all things in number and measure" (11:20). It was Augustine who gave the final stamp of approval to number symbolism. As a philosopher, he saw in number an image of the absolute and unchangeable. He reasoned as follows:

There is a relation of numbers which cannot possibly be impaired or altered, nor can any nature by any amount of violence prevent the number which comes after one from being the double of one. This can in no way be changed; and yet you represent God as changeable.[42]

[39]Book II:24:4, *Ibid.,* p. 395.

[40]*Hortatory Address to the Greeks,* Chap. 19, *Ibid.,* p. 280.

[41]Clement in *Stromata,* Chap. 6, *Ibid.,* Vol. 2, p. 452.

[42]*On the Morals of the Manichaeans,* 11:12, trans. Richard Stothert, *A Select Library of the Nicene and Post-Nicene Fathers of the Christian Church* (Buffalo: The Christian Literature Co., 1886), Vol. 4, p. 76.

There is no doubt that Augustine was caught up with the numerological speculations of Pythagoras and his successors. His view of the number 6 gives evidence of the source of influence for it is precisely the approach of Pythagoras.

> Six is a number perfect in itself, and not because God created all things in six days; rather the converse is true; God created all things in six days because this number is perfect and it would have been perfect even if the work of six days did not exist.[43]

Augustine devoted considerable space in his writings to the task of establishing meanings for certain numbers. Two was supposed to represent the "two-fold precept of love,"[44] 7 was the number of the Holy Spirit,[45] 10, the number of the law,[46] and 17, "grace supervening upon the law."[47]

The age of the Church Fathers saw rapid growth and development of numerological speculation. We should like to observe at this point that this development was not due to new realizations of the significance of Biblical theories and the speculations of the Gnostics.

The Middle Ages and the Renaissance (500–1600). The Middle Ages did not produce any new developments in the area of number symbolism, but it did expand those ideas already made popular. The dominant Medieval attitude was merely an elaboration of the numerology of Augustine and his predecessors. On the basis of Pythagorean and Gnostic theories, each number was assigned a root meaning and diversified representations. Some of the identifications were as follows: 1, unity of God and Spirit; 2, diversity of earth and matter; 4, extension of duality, earth; 5, flesh (senses); 6, earthly perfection (days of creation); 7, $(3 + 4)$ universe of spirit and matter; 8, immortality; 9,

---

[43]Quoted in Dantzig, *op. cit.,* p. 45.
[44]Philip Schaff, *op. cit.,* VI, p. 113.
[45]*Ibid.,* VI, p. 442. In his sermon on Mark 8:5 Augustine devotes much space to the symbolical implications of the number 7. (Cf. VI, p. 406 ff.
[46]*Ibid.,* VI, p. 51.
[47]*Ibid.,* VI, p. 442.

extension of trinity, angelic number; and 10, extension of unity, perfect completeness.[48]

Symbolic numbers and their meanings were not only a characteristic of Medieval Christian writings, but they also were prominent in the vast body of Kabbalistic literature of Jews.[49] The origin of much of this literature, according to Abba H. Silver, is to be traced to Babylon during the Geonic period (550—1000 A.D.).[50]

> At least two important Kabbalistic works were composed or edited there, the "Sefer Yetzirah" (the Book of Formation) on the creative powers of letters and numbers, and the "Shiur Komah" (The Measure of the Height) an anthropomorphic work on the dimensions of the Deity.[51]

Attempts were made in this literature to give every word and letter of the Scripture some special, mysterious meaning. Number symbolism was also a prominent feature of the Talmudic and Midrashic literature of the Jews.

The Middle Ages and Renaissance periods were fundamentally periods of numerological expansion of previously established ideas. The basis for these speculations was the mysteries of the Gnostics, the theories of Pythagoras and the polemics of the Fathers.

C. The Interpretation of Symbolic Numbers

Number symbolism and the Scriptures. The question which needs to be raised at this point relates to the problem of number symbolism and its employment in Scripture. As previously noted, there are some scholars who argue that there is no number symbolism in the Bible at all, or if there is, it is extremely limited.[52] Others are able to detect symbolism, in

---

[48]Vincent F. Hopper, "Number" *An Encyclopedia of Religion,* V. Ferm, ed. (New York: The Philosophical Library, 1945), p 755.

[49]Full discussion of the nature of this literature will be found on p. 131.

[50]"Kabbalah," *An Encyclopedia of Religion,* V. Ferm, ed. (New York: The Philosophical Library, 1945), p. 412.

[51]*Ibid.*

[52]*Supra,* p. 103-104.

most of the words and even the letters used in the Bible. It is the view of this writer that the only number used symbolically in the Scripture to any degree with discernible significance, is the number 7. The number seven occurs in one way or another in nearly six hundred passages in the Bible.[53] L. A. Muirhead feels that:

> In regard to 7, the ritual arrangements found in the Pentateuch would alone warrant the conclusion that this number was regarded as in some sense sacred. If we read that God blessed the 7th day and sanctified it (Gen. 2:3), and find that peculiar religious observances or customs with a religious basis attached, not only to the 7th day, but to the 7th month, the 7th year, and the 7 x 7th year, we seem warranted in saying that, among the people of the Bible, 7 represents a mystic cycle of work and rest, within which God both accomplishes His purpose in the universe and cooperates with sanctified men.[54]

There are a number of reasons for the conclusion that seven constitutes the only significant and meaningful symbolic number in Scripture. First, this is the only number which appears to be used symbolically with any consistency in contemporary extra-biblical literature. It should be remembered that the Bible was not written in a cultural or literary vacuum. The Old Testament accurately reflects literary practices of its day. This is not to say that its theology is a borrowed theology, but it does recognize the fact that the distinctive theological truths of the Bible were written in the language of its day, employing well-known idioms and literary devices. The use of the number 7 symbolically was a common phenomenon among the nations surrounding ancient Israel. As early as the time of Abraham (c. 2000 B.C.) the number seven was employed symbolically. According to Smith the number seven:

> . . . is found in reference to ritual in the age of Gudea. . . . "Seven gods" at the end of an enumeration meant "all the gods . . ."[55]

---

[53]Smith, op. cit., p. 2159.
[54]"Numbers," Dictionary of the Apostolic Church, ed., James Hastings (New York: Charles Scribners Sons, 1918), p. 92.
[55]Smith, op. cit., p. 2159.

It appears in Sumerican epic tales and myths[56] and in the Assyrian version of "The Epic of Gilgamesh."[57] Ritualistically it appears in a Hittite "Ritual Against Domestic Quarrel." Lines 25-31 read as follows:

> She then waves them over them and speaks as follows: "Let the tongues of these days be cut off! Let the words of these days be cut off! And she throws them into the hearth.
> Afterward the Old Woman takes a tray and places *seven* tongues and *seven* hands . . . upon it . . .[58]

The Amarna letters provide numerous examples of this phenomenon. In a letter from Rib-Addi, prince of Byblos, to Akh-en-Aton the following lines appear:

> Rib-Ad [di spoke] to the king, [his] lor[d, the Sun-god of the lands.] Beneath the feet [of the king, my lord,] *seven times, and seven times* [I fall.][59]

A good number of the Amarna letters, written at different times, from different kings use the same expression.[60] The idiom employed in these letters is most interesting in the light of Genesis 33:3. When Jacob met Esau:

> . . . he passed over before them, and bowed himself to the ground seven times, until he came near to his brother (KJV).

In Ugaritic mythology the number seven is used with regularity for symbolic purposes. In the "Tale of Aqhat" it is primarily used with reference to time periods such as "seventh day"[61] and

---

[56]"Gilgamesh and the Land of the Living," trans. S. N. Kramer, *ANET*, p. 48, lines 36, 62; "Inanna's Descent to the Nether World" *Ibid.*, pp. 54, 55. lines 100, 116, 122, 156.

[57]*ANET*, p. 82, Tablet IV, line 45; p. 87, Tablet VII:iv:10.

[58]"Ritual Against Domestic Quarrel" trans. Albrecht Goetze, *ANET*, p. 350, (italics mine).

[59]The Amarna Letters, trans. W. F. Albright, *ANET*, p. 483, Letter no. 137, lines 1-5 (italics mine).

[60]*Ibid.*, p. 484, Letter no. 147, lines 1-5; p. 485, Letter no. xix, p. 100, lines 5-10; Letter no. 250, lines 1-5, etc.

[61]*ANET*, trans. H. L. Ginsberg, p. 150, AQHT A:i:13,16.

"seven years."[62] Concerning the ritualistic practices of the king
at Ugarit we read:

> [To] the places of the gods he goes on foot,
> The king shall go on foot
> Seven times to all of them (UT 5:24-26).[63]

There appears to be little doubt that the contemporaries of
the Biblical writers used the number quite freely in a symbolical
manner. In all cases it seems that the idea conveyed is that of
"completeness."

In the Old Testament, the employment of the number seven,
from a literary standpoint, seems to be similar to that of contemporary inscriptions. It is used commonly in historical narratives,
e.g., Jacob's 7 years' service for Rachel (Gen. 29:20 f.); 7 years
of plenty and 7 years of famine (Gen. 41:53); Samson's 7 day
marriage feast (Judg. 14:12; cf. Gen. 29:27);[64] the 7 daughters
of Jethro (Exod. 2:16); 7 sons of Jesse (I Sam. 16:10); 7 sons of
Saul (II Sam. 21:6); etc.[65] Ritualistically, its use is also common. Compare for example the 7 days of unleavened bread
(Exod. 34:18), the 7 days of the Feast of Tabernacles (Lev.
23:34); the 7th year as the sabbatical year (Exod. 21:2); the
7 he-lambs of the Mosaic law (Num. 28:11, 19, 27; etc.). The
requirement for Naaman to dip in the Jordan 7 times (II
Kings 5:10); and 7 altars, 7 bullocks, and 7 rams of Balak
(Num. 23:1, 14, 29).[66] A large number of the uses of seven
are commonly identified as "didactic" or a literary use of seven.[67]
The sevenfold curse predicted for the murder of Cain (Gen.
4:15); fleeing 7 days (Deut. 28:7, 25); deliverance from 7 trou-

[62]*Ibid.,* p. 153, AQHT C:i:30, and iv:176.

[63]A. F. Rainey, "The Kingdom of Ugarit" *The Biblical Archaeologist,*
Vol. 28 (Dec. 1965), p. 119.

[64]Cf. also Judges 16:9, 7.

[65]Also Job 1:2; 42:13; Josh. 6:8 ff.; I Kings 18:43 f.; II Kings 4:35;
Dan. 4:16, 23, 25, 32; Matt. 15:34-36; 22:25; Mark 16:9; Luke 2:36; 8:2;
Acts 7:3 ff.; etc.

[66]Also Exod. 22:30; 29:30, 35, 37; Lev. 16:14, 19; 14:7; 16, 27; 12:3;
Num. 8:2; Zech. 4:2; etc.

[67]Smith, *op. cit.,* p. 2160.

bles (Job 5:19); praise of God 7 times a day (Ps. 119:164); and 7 fold purification of silver (Ps. 12:6).[68] The final class of "sevens" found in the Bible is generally classified as "apocalyptic." They appear primarily in the Book of Revelation and since they were previously discussed, we shall not consider the subject any further.

It is generally agreed that the fundamental idea conveyed by the symbolic use of seven is that of "completeness" or "perfection." This conclusion is not based on the sum of any of its factors or any other arithmetical feature of the number, but its *usus loquendi.*[69]

Analysis of significant numbers in Scripture. If seven is the only important symbolic number in Scripture, how shall one regard the repetitious use of other numbers in the Bible? This is an important question and demands a satisfactory answer. As previously stated, it is the view of this writer that the only number used symbolically in the Scripture to any degree with *discernible significance* is the number seven. It should be pointed out that nowhere in Scripture is any number given any specific theological or mystical meaning! This appears to be rather strange if all numbers such as 1, 2, 3, 4, 5, 10, 12, 40, etc. are really symbols. It is a well-known fact that, generally, when the Bible employs a symbol, it either explains the significance of that symbol in the immediate context (e.g., the candlestick and stars of Revelation) or in some other part of Scripture. Nowhere in Scripture, however, is there the slightest hint that numbers are employed symbolically, nor are we told what their theological meaning might be.[70] Whatever has been deduced on this subject has been pure speculation and the result subjective reasoning. The number three, for example, is a number which is regarded by many as an important symbolic number. However, opinion on this conclusion is far from unanimous. John D. Davis states that "three had apparently no symbolism;

---

[68]Also Deut. 28:7, 25; Ruth 4:15; I Sam. 2:5; Ps. 79:12.

[69]See John D. Davis, *op. cit.,* p. 546 who argues for the same view.

[70]Revelation 13:18 declares the number 666 to be symbolical, but it does not attach any theological value to the letters. It is merely a symbol for the anti-christ.

but emphasis was conventionally expressed by it . . ."[71] Gerald
T. Kennedy also draws the same conclusion after careful study
of the number and its uses in the Bible.[72]

If one would take all the occurrences of this number in the
Bible, he could find any number of symbolical meanings for
the number because it is employed in a variety of manners.
Scripture does not give it specific theological value and therefore inductive reasoning must be employed. In fact, commentators are agreed that this is the only way in which one may
discover the meanings of numbers.[73] Milton S. Terry points out
that:

> The only valid method of ascertaining the symbolical meaning
> and usage of such numbers, names, and colours in the Scriptures,
> is by an ample collation and study of the passages where they
> occur. The hermeneutical process is therefore essentially the
> same as that by which we ascertain the "usus loquendi" of
> words, and the province of hermeneutics is, not to furnish an
> elaborate discussion of the subject, but to exhibit the principles
> and methods by which such discussion should be carried out.[74]

What is not explained, however, is that which actually constitutes "ample collation and study." The only real "ample collation" is one which considers every occurrence of a number
and it is difficult to see how any specific conclusions could possibly be reached with several hundred occurrences of a number
in as many different contexts and situations. When all the occurrences of the number three are studied, the most one could
say for its symbolism is that it conveys the idea of "completeness."[75] This number may have conveyed this concept because of the nature of common triads with which everyone
was familiar:

---

[71]*Op. cit.*, p. 546.

[72]"The Use of Numbers in Sacred Scripture," *American Ecclesiastical Review*, LXXXIX (July, 1958), p. 27.

[73]A. Berkeley Mickelson, *Interpreting the Bible* (Grand Rapids: Wm. B. Eerdmans Publishing Co., 1963), p. 272.

[74]*Biblical Hermeneutics* (Grand Rapids: Zondervan Publishing House, n.d.), p. 380.

[75]This is precisely the conclusion of Pope, *op. cit.*, p. 564.

Beginning	Middle	End
Father	Mother	Child
Heaven	Earth	Sea
Morning	Noon	Night
Right	Middle	Left

If one would examine the writings of popular interpreters however, he would be amazed at the variety of theological truths this little number is supposed to convey. J. Edwin Hartill, for example, says that three is the number of ". . . union, approval, approbation, co-ordination, completeness, and perfection."[76] He provides only thirty to forty proofs for this conclusion which is interesting in the light of the fact that the number three occurs over 450 times in the Bible. Terry, on the other hand, feels that the number means "Divine fulness in unity, the number of God."[77] Lange, after study of the number, concludes that it signifies "Life, spirit, new life, resurrection, unclean spirits, etc."[78] One could very easily multiply examples of the various meanings given to this number. It appears that there are almost as many different interpretations of the number as there are interpreters. What has been observed with regard to the interpretation of the number three can be observed with the rest of the numbers. The reader is referred to the table on page 122, for a comparison of the meanings for so-called symbolic numbers.

The system of symbolic numbers, as used in the Christian church must be regarded as a post-Apostolic development. Most of the meanings adopted today for the symbolic numbers are those that were proposed by the Church Fathers.[79] And one should remember that Augustine, along with the other fathers, was strongly influenced by the early Gnostic heresies and Pythagorean theories with regard to symbolic numerology. It is

[76]*Op. cit.*, p. 111.

[77]*Op. cit.*, p. 381.

[78]*Revelation, Commentary on the Holy Scriptures*, ed. by Philip Schaff, pp. 14-16.

[79]The number forty is usually regarded as meaning "a period of judgment." Cf. Terry, *op. cit.*, p. 385, and Hartill, *op. cit.*, p. 121. Augustine in a letter written about A.D. 400 argues that forty means "life of toil and self control." Letter LV:15:28, Philip Schaff, *op. cit.*, I, p. 312.

rather interesting that not one New Testament writer ever
pointed back to the significance of a symbolic number occurring
in the Old Testament. This seems rather strange if the phenom-

TABLE VI

THE INTERPRETATIONS OF SYMBOLIC NUMBERS

NUMBER	HARTILL[80]	TERRY[81]
One	Independence, the number of God.	Unity
Two	Division, separation	-------------------
Three	Union, approval, approbation, coordination, perfection, etc.	Divine fulness in unity, the number of God.
Four	Creation refers to the earth	World, creation.
Five	God's grace.	-------------------
Six	Number of man.	-------------------
Seven	Fulness, perfection, completeness.	Sacred number of the covenant between God and man.
Eight	Resurrection	-------------------
Nine	Judgment, finality, completion	-------------------
Ten	Perfection or completeness in divine order.	Fulness, completeness.
Twelve	Governmental perfection or rule.	Mystical number of God's chosen people.
Forty	Probation, testing or trial.	Period of judgment.
Seventy	-------------------	Time of judgment of God's people.

[80]*Op. cit.*, pp. 109-123.
[81]*Op. cit.*, pp. 380-384.

NUMBER	LANGE[82]	GUNNER[83]
One	Unity	Unity
Two	Revelation, harmonious contrast, discord, war ruin, death, etc.	Unity and division
Three	Life, spirit, new life resurrection, unclean spirits, etc.	Trinity of persons in the Godhead, God's mighty acts.
Four	Space, the world.	Symbol of completion.
Five	$(2 + 3)$ — life moved by the spirit, hand, action, freedom, folly, etc.	Completeness.
Six	$(3 \times 2, 2 \times 3)$ struggle between spirit and nature endless toil, holy operations, etc.	Number of man.
Seven	Completed work, rest full development.	Completion, fulfilment
Eight	The number of the double world of the cosmos, in antithesis of Heaven and earth.	....
Nine	(3×3) perfect movement of spirit, of renewal.	....
Ten	$(5 + 5)$ completed course of time.	....
Twelve	(3×4) number of the spirit world, plentitude, etc.	The elective purposes of God.
Forty	....	Development of history, associated with salvation.
Seventy	....	God's administration of the world.

[82]*Op. cit.*, pp. 14-16.
[83]*Op. cit.*, pp. 897-898.

enon was so apparent. Many other types and symbols are alluded to in the New Testament and explained, but never numbers.

It should also be pointed out that the Old and New Testaments contain some 2000 years of history (from Abraham to John) which contain an abundance of statistical and chronological data. With that much material it is not difficult to select a number occurring in similar circumstances and assign a mystical or theological meaning to it. This, in fact, could be done with considerable ease with the *Congressional Record!*

D. Summary

After analyzing available data on the antiquity of symbolic numbers it was shown that: (1) Symbolic or significant numbers were used prior to the time of Moses and were common literary phenomena among his contemporaries; (2) When numbers were used symbolically they only conveyed general concepts (e.g., completeness, fulness, etc.); (3) The number seven is the only number which *clearly* shows symbolic usage in the Bible and the concepts it conveys are those that are common to contemporary texts; (4) The exegetical method of ascribing theological values to numbers is of Greek origin and finds its development primarily among the Gnostics, Neo-Pythagoreans, and Jewish allegorists. The Christianization of this system was a Post-Apostolic development pursued mainly by the Church Fathers.

It is our conclusion that the mystical or symbolical interpretation of numbers has little place in a sound system of hermeneutics.

Chapter 6

THE MYSTICAL USE OF NUMBERS

The theory of mystical numbers is that system of interpretation which endeavors to seek out hidden truths by means of numerical phenomena. This system operates upon the basic premise that the Bible, like the universe, exhibits numerical and symmetrical design because it was created by God. It is argued that all God does He does with perfection and precision. His works are "absolutely perfect in every particular."[1] All His works are perfect in power, holiness, design, execution, object, end, and perfect in number.[2] According to this theory, the perfection of God's handiwork is in evidence in both His works and words.[3] If one is to really understand the world around him, he must seek out the grand mysteries in nature as they are revealed in numeric design. It is the same with the Word of God. The key to understanding its truth and the secret to unlocking its problems is the study of its numerical design. A careful study of these numeric patterns, according to this theory, will give the student insights into Scriptures which he could get in no other way.

The system of Biblical numerics operates on the basis of two basic assumptions. First, there is *design* in the use of numbers (both open and hidden) in Scripture. Secondly, there is *symbolical* or *theological significance* connected with the numerical patterns found in the Bible.

A. Historical Survey of the Concept of Mystical Numbers

Origin and early development. The origin of mystical numerology is not clear from historical sources, but it appears that its origin is like that of number symbolism.[4] According to Bell

---

[1]E. W. Bullinger, *Number in Scripture* (London: Eyre & Spottiswoode Ltd., 1913), p. 1.

[2]*Ibid.*

[3]*Ibid.*, p. 2.

[4]Supra, p. 108 ff.

"numerology was born the hour Pythagoras discovered the law of musical intervals."[5] While the principal development of this system can be traced to this man, there is some evidence that the idea was known earlier. Hopper cites evidence that the Babylonians had some knowledge of the idea of Gematria[6] during the time of Sargon II. The wall at Khorsabad was supposed to have been built according to the numerical value of Sargon's name.[7] Examples of Gematria are found in early Greek mythology also. The names of the heroes Patroclus, Hector and Achilles add up to 87, 1225 and 1276 respectively. To this was attributed the superiority of Achilles. An ancient poet desiring to confound his pet enemy, whose name was Thamagoras, proved that the word was equivalent to *loimos,* a sort of pestilence.[8] The real organization and development of the system of mystical numbers must however, be attributed to Pythagoras. In fact, when he returned from travel and study in Babylon and Egypt, he founded a secret cult in southern Italy based on numerical explanations for the phenomena of the universe. According to Pythagoras:

> All things are fittingly ordered according to the nature of numbers; number is the eternal essence; God is number; number is God.[9]

The Pythagorean philosophy contained the fundamental idea that only through number and form can man grasp the nature of the universe. Such thoughts were expressed by Philolaus, Pythagoras' ablest disciple and also by Nicomachus, who is usually considered a neo-Pythagorean:

> All things which can be known have a number; for it is not possible that without number anything can be either conceived or known (Philolaus).

---

[5]E. T. Bell, *Numerology* (New York: The Century Co., 1933), p. 81.

[6]The interpretation of a word according to the numerical value of its letters.

[7]Hopper, *op. cit.,* p. 62.

[8]See Dantzig, *op. cit.,* p. 39.

[9]Quoted by Bell, *op. cit.,* p. 84.

All things that have been arranged by nature according to a workman-like plan appear, both individually and as a whole, as singled out and set in order by Foreknowledge and Reason, which created all according to number, conceivable to mind only and therefore wholly immaterial; yet real; indeed, the really real, the eternal (Nicomachus).[10]

The Pythagoreans considered numbers to be the elements and origin of everything. It was their view that numeral symbols preceded all other forms of writing. This is what they really meant when they said: "Numbers by nature are the first and prior to all things" (Aristotle's *Metaphysics*, Book I, chap. 5). The letters of the earliest alphabet having been numeral symbols, all words were originally made up of numeral symbols or numbers.[11] According to the *Sefer Yezira*[12] and the Pythagoreans, the four elements, fire, air, water, earth, emanated from the first four numbers, I, II, III, IV.

There is little doubt that the early origin and development of the idea of mystical and symbolical numerology should be traced to Pythagoras and his followers. Like number symbolism, Gematria was popularized in Palestine among the Jews by means of Greek influence. There is no evidence that Gematria was ever employed by Biblical writers with the possible exception of the reference to the anti-christ in Revelation 13:18.[13] Casper Levias is quite convinced of this fact:

In the Bible itself there is no reference to numerical gematria, or the symbolic use of numbers, and their existence cannot be positively demonstrated.[14]

The possibility of Biblical Gematria is discussed below with special consideration of modern applications.[15]

Mystical numerology and the Church Fathers. With the

---

[10]Quoted in Dantzig, *op. cit.*, p. 43.
[11]A view which this writer rejects, see above, p. 30 ff.
[12]A book in the Jewish Kabbala dating from the 9th cent. A.D.
[13]Full discussion of this verse may be found on p. 144.
[14]"Gematria" *The Jewish Encyclopedia* (New York: Funk and Wagnalls Co., 1903), p. 589.
[15]See p. 142 f.

rise of the Gnostic heresies came the concomitant growth of the pseudo-science of Gematria. While Biblical writers do not employ the system, the Church Fathers were profoundly influenced by it, so much so, that they made it part of their apologetic. On the other hand, some of the Fathers were severe critics of the system and the results it yielded. Augustine reflects the general point of view of his times which was favorable to this system of exegesis.

> Ignorance of numbers, too, prevents us from understanding things that are set down in Scripture in a figurative and mystical way. A candid mind, if I may so speak, cannot but be anxious, for example, to ascertain what is meant by the fact that Moses and Elijah, and our Lord Himself, all fasted for forty days.[16]

It was the view of Hermippus that mystical numerology originated with the Jews from which Pythagoras copied it. Origen writes:

> It is said, moreover, that Hermippus has recorded in his first book, *On Lawgivers*, that it was from the Jewish people that Pythagoras derived the philosophy which he introduced among the Greeks.[17]

Many of the Fathers show considerable knowledge of the ideas of Pythagoras and refer to him by name on a number of occasions.[18] Methodius was strongly influenced by him and gives evidence of this in *The Banquet of the Ten Virgins*.

> For a thousand, consisting of a hundred multiplied by ten, embraces a full and perfect number, and is a symbol of the Father Himself, who made the universe by Himself and rules all

---

[16]Christian Doctrine II, XVI. Quoted in James Wood, *The Interpretation of the Bible* (London: Gerald Duckworth and Co., Ltd., 1958), p. 67.

[17]*Against Celsus*, Book I, chap. XV, Alexander Roberts and James Donaldson, eds., *The Ante-Nicene Fathers*, p. 402.

[18]Hippolytus, *The Refutation of All Heresies*, Book I, chap. XVI, *Ibid.*, V, p. 81 ff.
Arnobius, *Against the Heathen*, Book II, Par. 10, *Ibid.*, VI, pp. 437, 424.
Lactantius, *The Divine Institutes*, Book I, chap. V. *Ibid.*, VII, p. 14.

things for Himself. Two hundred embraces two perfect numbers united together, and is the symbol of the Holy Spirit, since
He is the author of our knowledge of the number six pro-
ceeding from unity is composed of its proper parts, so that
nothing in it is wanting, and is complete when resolved into
its parts.[19]

Methodius, like many of the Fathers, rejected the conclusions of
the Gnostics and the Jewish mythologies of his day, but was
much impressed with potency of numerology as an apologetic.
The Gnostics and Jews were in turn influenced by the Pythagoreans and Neo-Pythagoreans of days gone by. The influence
of Pythagoras shows up in his interest in the number six. This
was considered a "perfect number" by the Pythagoreans because
it equalled the sum of its own divisors.[20] The number six was
also a "triangular number" which was of great significance to the
ancients.[21] It was the view of Methodius and Augustine that
God completed the creation of the world on the sixth day simply
because six was a perfect number:

> Moreover, it is evident that the creation of the world was
> accomplished in harmony with this number, God having made
> heaven and earth, and the things which are in them, in six
> days; the word of creative power containing the number six,
> in accordance with which the Trinity is the maker of bodies.[22]

> Six is a number perfect in itself, and not because God created
> all things in six days; rather the converse is true; God created
> all thing in six days because this number is perfect, and it
> would have been perfect even if the work of the six days did
> not exist.[23]

---

[19]Methodius, *The Banquet of the Ten Virgins,* chap. XI, *Ibid.,* VI,
p. 339.

[20]The concept of "perfect" numbers is discussed on p. 108 of this book.

[21]A "triangular number" is one which can be reduced to a triangle of
dots. For example, $3 = \therefore$, $6 = \because\therefore$, etc. This phenomenon was represented by
the formula $\dfrac{x^2 + x}{2}$. Each side of the triangle contains an equal number

of units, the sum of which amounts to the number.

[22]Methodius, *The Banquet of the Ten Virgins,* chap. XI, *op. cit.,* VI,
p. 339.

[23]Quoted in Dantzig, *op. cit.,* p. 45.

It should not be supposed that all the Fathers were sympathetic
to the numerological calculations of their contemporaries. Irenaeus is an outstanding example of one who made valiant attempts to stem the tide of theological mysticism and allegorical interpretation which was popular in the early church. He
recognized the dangers of such a system both as to method and
result. He saw clearly that the method employed in this system
was quite subjective and, therefore, of no value:

> For choosing out of the law whatever things agree with the
> number adopted in their system, they thus violently strive to
> obtain proofs of its validity.[24]

Irenaeus traced the practices of mystical numbers in general
and Gematria in particular, back to the Greeks and says, in effect, that it has no place in Christian hermeneutics.[25]

> This very thing, too, still further demonstrates their opinion
> false, and their fictitious system untenable; that they endeavor
> to bring forward proofs of it, sometimes through means of
> numbers, and the syllables of names, sometimes also through
> the letters of syllables, and yet again through those numbers,
> which are, according to the practice followed by the Greeks,
> contained in different letters: this I say, demonstrates in the
> clearest manner their overthrow and confusion, as well as the
> untenable and perverse character of their professed knowl-
> edge.[26]

In the same composition, Irenaeus points out that in the study
of numerics long hours were spent analyzing and praising the
work of the artist (the Lord) and this was done to the neglect
of the artist himself.[27] The observations of Irenaeus are worth
noting at this point because interpreters today have adopted
methods of interpretation which are the same as the Gnostics
of the early centuries of church history. The advice and warn-
ings of this church father have their practical application, therefore, not only in ancient times, but in our present situation.

24*Against Heresies,* Book II, chap. 24, par. 3, *op. cit.,* I, p. 394.
25A view which this writer shares without qualification.
26*Against Heresies,* Book II, chap. 24, par. 1, *op. cit.,* I, p. 393.
27*Ibid.,* p. 396.

Mystical numerology in the Middle Ages and Renaissance
(A.D. 500—A.D. 1600). During the Middle Ages interest in
mystical numerology not only grew in Christian circles, but it
caught the fancy of Jewish writers. The Cabala,[28] a collec-
tion of writings exhibiting the esoteric doctrines of Judaism from
the ninth century A.D onward, shows that Jewish thinkers were
quite preoccupied with the idea of mystical numerics. The
fundamental doctrines of the Cabala were derived from Hellenistic Judaism, Neo-Platonism and Neo-Pythagoreanism, with
some trace of Gnosticism.[29] The writers of the Cabalistic literature were convinced that there was a deeper meaning to
Scripture than just the literal interpretation of the text. They regarded the letters, words, and names of the Bible as possessed of deeply hidden divine mysteries. In their endeavor to
unlock the deep mysteries of Scripture, they employed a system
of exegesis which would yield the desired results. The chief
system was that of Gematria. As early as the *Sefer Yezirah*
(ninth cent.) the system of Gematria was employed with regularity. The first Mishnah of *Sefer Yezirah* reads as follows:
"Thirty-two mysterious ways has the Lord, the Lord of hosts, ordained through Scribe, Script and Scroll."[30] The thirty-two
mysterious ways are the twenty-two letters of the Hebrew
alphabet, which represent thirty-two sounds. In accordance with
the belief of the ancients that the letters of the alphabet were
of divine origin, the *Sefer Yetzirah* explains that the thirty-two
ways of wisdom were ordained by God through the *sopēr*
(scribe), the man whom God inspired to invent the alphabet,
sāpûr (script), the letters, and *sēper* (scroll), the material on
which the letters were displayed.[31] In the Cabala, four systems of exegesis were prominent. *Gematria,* or the interpretation
of a word according to the numerical value of its letters was

---

[28]The term *qblh* is from *qbl* "to receive." The Cabala, therefore, was
considered the "received or traditional lore."

[29]August Wünsche, "Cabala," *The New Schaff-Herzog Religious Encyclopedia,* Samuel M. Jackson, ed., II, p. 326.

[30]Translation of: פְלִיאוֹת   נְתִיבוֹת   וּשְׁתַּיִם   שְׁלֹשִׁים
וְסֵפֶר   וְסִפּוּר   בְּסוֹפֵר   צְבָאוֹת   יהוה   יה   חקק

[31]For a detailed discussion of this doctrine see Louis Ginzberg, "Cabala,"
op. cit., III, p. 456 ff.

perhaps the most common. *Notarikon*, the taking each letter of
a word as the initial of some other word, was also freely employed. The third system was called *temurah* or the substituting
of one letter for another. Finally, the system of *tziruf* or the
transposing of letters was used.

By the use of Gematria, the Cabala established many hidden
relationships between various words of the Bible. The significance of the word "amen" was combined with "Jehovah Adoni"
because they both equaled 91 numerically. The meanings of
certain numbers were also established on the basis of their appearance in certain words. The number thirteen, for example,
was contained in the word *'ḥd* or "unity." It was also contained
in *'hbh* "love." Therefore, the number thirteen was thought to
signify "love of unity."

According to the Cabala, objects could be identified by letter
clusters. For example, it was proposed that the nose and eyes
were represented in the group of letters *yoḏ, waw, yoḏ*.

The Cabala reflects what can be considered as normative
exegesis in the Middle Ages, both in Jewish and Christian circles.
Both were influenced by Gnosticism and Pythagorean numerology and approached Scripture allegorically.

Mystical numerology occupied the attention of scholars during
the days of Luther and was employed as an apologetic just as
it was in the days of the Church Fathers. Peter Bungus, who
lived in the days of Luther, wrote a book on numerology consisting of nearly seven hundred pages. A great part of this
work was devoted to the mystical 666, which he had found
equivalent to the name of Luther. In reply, Luther interpreted
666 as the forecast of the duration of the Papal regime.[32]

Mystical numerology and the modern era (1600-1966). In
modern times, the theory of mystical numerology or "Bible Numerics," as it is called today, has had many ardent advocates.
In 1863 a book entitled *Palmoni or The Numbers of Scripture*
gained considerable popularity and was responsible for initiating
new studies in this area.[33] The most energetic student of the

---

[32]Dantzig, *op. cit.*, pp. 39-40.
[33]M. Maham, *Palmoni or The Numerals of Scripture* (New York: D.
Appleton and Co., 1863).

system of Bible numerics was Ivan Panin.[34] He was a Russian by birth but when compelled to leave his country went to Germany and thence to America. He was a graduate of Harvard University and claimed to be an agnostic. After his conversion, he became very intrigued with the study of numbers for he felt that in this he had found irrefutable proof of the inspiration of the Bible. Contemporary with Panin in this venture was the well-known E. W. Bullinger of Great Britain.[35] Since the time of these men, little has been developed in this area, but books have appeared which propagate their ideas and expand their systems.[36]

The thing that is of special interest, however, is the gross silence in works of the above men concerning the origin of their exegetical systems. No credit is ever given to Pythagoras, the Talmudic or Cabalastic literature from which their methodology is derived. In fact, as one reads their works, he is constantly reminded of the fact that what they are proposing is new and unique. No man ever saw it until they brought it to light. In the introduction to a series of articles by Ivan Panin we are told that his numerological analysis is:

> . . . a secret which was concealed from all other men, including, it may be, the very writers of the Old Testament and New Testament books. . . .[37]

LeBaron W. Kinney, in the preface of his book on this subject, has this to say with regard to his discoveries in relation to the work of others:

> Others have shown there is design in the numbers, while we have tried to bring before the reader that doctrines and truths

---

[34]"Bible Numerics" *Things to Come* XVII, XVIII (1911-1912).

[35]*Number in Scripture* (London: Eyre and Spottiswoode, 1894; reprinted 1967 by Kregel Publications, Grand Rapids).

[36]R. McCormack, *Seven in Scripture* (London: Marshall Brothers, Limited, 1926).

LeBaron W. Kinney, *The Greatest Thing in the Universe* (New York: Loizeux Brothers, 1939).

Karl G. Sabiers, *Astounding New Discoveries* (Los Angeles: Robertson Publishing Company, 1941).

[37]*Things to Come,* XVII (Jan. 1911), No. 1, p. 2.

are woven into these designs. Mr. Grant in his *Numerical Bible* comes nearer to our method than any other writer. He does not, however, bring in the numerical value of the letters. *We believe we have discovered basic meanings that were not known before.*[38]

The same extravagant claims are made by Karl G. Sabiers in his book *Astounding New Discoveries.*[39] It would seem that out of intellectual honesty these men would at least discuss the development of the system of numerics by the Pythagoreans, the early exegesis of Jews and Gnostics, and the writings of the Church Fathers. What is proposed by these writers is not new at all and one gets the impression that they attempt to completely hide the origin of their methodology lest they fall under the same condemnation as the allegorizing Gnostics in the days of Irenaeus. Kinney, for example, pleads with the reader that he not associate the patterns found in Biblical numbers with what is known as "numerology."[40] I would assume that by "numerology" he means the exegetical methods of the early Jews and Gnostics. But we should like to propose that if there is really a difference between his numerology and that of the Gnostics it has yet to be demonstrated. The mathematical procedures are precisely those of the Pythagoreans and the Gnostics. The only difference is that the conclusions are changed in order to conform to Christian theology.

B. Supposed Values of Bible (mystical) Numerics

Bible numerics provides Christian growth. According to the advocates of this system of exegesis, if one applies himself to the study of Biblical numbers he can greatly enrich his faith. Kinney writes:

> The types and numbers of Scripture are a Divine secret code language, by which to those who love His Word enough to search it, God may reveal things that are very precious.[41]

---

[38]*Op. cit.*, p. 13 (italics mine).
[39]*Op. cit.*, pp. 7, 8, 13, etc.
[40]*Op. cit.*, p. 11.
[41]*Op. cit.*, p. 30.

There is no doubt that these men are earnest in attempting to help God's people to stand against the critical attacks on the Bible and to grow in the faith, but it is highly questionable whether a study of numbers can accomplish this. Nowhere in Scripture is this method of study referred to or suggested as a key to understanding the Bible.

Bible numerics secures the perfect text of the Bible. It was the view of Panin that the original text of Scripture could be reconstructed on the basis of numerical patterns:

> Now, however, a perfect text can be obtained. The key of "Bible Numerics" detects at once the true: . . .[42]

It, also, was the view of Panin that when seven and its multiples appear as numeric patterns of a text, it must be the original.

Bible numerics provide the solution to authorship problems — According to Panin:

> Numerics solve the problem of New Testament authorship as here presented; and every one of the 33 Bible writers can be demonstrated as surely as those eight New Testament writers to be presented in our next paper.[43]

Bible numerics prove the inspiration of the Bible. In the book *Astounding New Discoveries* there is consistent mention of the fact that the "discovery" of numerics is the final and irrefutable proof of the divine inspiration of the Bible. It is argued that numerics ". . . are facts which scientifically prove that the Bible could not possibly have been written by mere human beings alone, but that it was a supernatural, God inspired, God given book."[44] Panin argued for the same idea:

> The present writer's labours in the field of numerics have been numerous and arduous, but they have not been desultory; the

---

[42]*Op. cit.,* XVII (1911), No. 1, p. 2.

[43]*Ibid.,* XIX (1913), No. 1, p. 7. Cf. also Vol. 18, (Feb. 1912), No. 2, p. 21. A more recent attempt to prove authorship with the use of numbers (and a computer) is that of Rev. A. Q. Morton. See Reinier Schippers, "Paul and the Computer" *Christianity Today,* Dec. 4 ,1964, p. 7 ff.

[44]Karl G. Sabiers, *op. cit.,* p. 7. Cf. also pp. 8, 9, 11, 13, etc.

reason being that he desired first of all to establish before the candid reader the fact that the unique, and on purely human grounds, inexplicable numeric structure of Scripture establishes its being the writing not of the human mind, but of a super-human mind.[45]

Evaluation of these claims will not be undertaken at this point, but will be given along with an evaluation of the methodology of this system.

C. Methodology Employed in the Analysis of Mystical Numbers

Open numeric phenomena. The open numeric phenomena are the data of the Biblical text which exhibit numeric structures which are supposed to be plain and incontestable. The numer-ological patterns of this class are sought out by two principal methods: First, there is the numeric analysis of verses and sen-tences. This consists of the counting of: (1) the number of letters in a verse, (2) the number of words in a sentence, and (3) the number of significant words. Panin's treatment of Genesis 1:1 is a good example of this method:

> The number of words in this verse in the Hebrew, in which the Old Testament is written, is seven. (Feature 1) These seven words have fourteen syllables, or 2 sevens (Feature 2), and 28 letters, or 4 sevens (Feature 3).

> The 28 letters of these seven words are thus divided: the first three words constituting the subject and predicate of the sen-tence — "In the beginning God created" — have 14 letters, or 2 sevens; the last four words, constituting the object of the sentence — "The heavens and the earth" — have also 14 letters (Feature 4).

> The object of the sentence contained in the last four words consists of separate objects: "the heavens and the earth." Ac-cordingly, the 14 letters constituting the words of this object of the sentence are in their turn thus divided: The first object, "the heavens," has seven letters; the second object "and the earth," has also seven (Feature 5).[46]

[45]*Op. cit.*, XVIII, No. 2, p. 20.
[46]*Op. cit.*, XVII, No. 12, p. 140.

The emphasis upon the number seven and its multiples is supposed to be a proof that the text is Divinely inspired and perfectly preserved. Oswald T. Allis correctly observes that such reasoning is false and with good reason:

> If the fact that verse 1 is a perfect example of 7's appearing in both words and letters means that its text has been perfectly preserved, are we to infer that verse 2 has been imperfectly transmitted to us because it has 52 letters? Or does this verse have a different numeric structure?[47]

With a little ingenuity and patience one can find multiples of seven or any other number in any document. This summer, for example, while working on the translation of a fifth century B.C. Aramaic document it was discovered that a number of sevens and its multiples were present. The opening sentence reads as follows:

בֵּ|ן לכסלו הו יום / למסורע שנת \\ / \\ /
ארתחשסש מלכא אמר מחסיה.

"On the 21st of Chisleu, that is the 1st day of Mesore, the 6th year of Artaxerxes, [the] king, said Mahseiah." Careful analysis brought the following numerical data to light. The sentence contained 49 letters and signs which is 7 sevens (Feature 1). The first numerical sign in the verse was | ‌ٮ or 21. This is the same as 7 x 3 (Feature 2). The dateline of the letter includes three numbers and the smallest time unit (day) and the largest time unit (year) are 1 and 6 respectively. The total is seven (Feature 3). When all the numerals of the sentence are added together the total is 28 or 4 sevens (Feature 4). The sentence contains only 7 sibilants (ס and ש) (Feature 5), etc.

If the reasoning of the advocates of mystical numerology is correct, then we should regard the *Conveyance Document* of 460 B.C. as divinely inspired.[48]

Not only are words of a single verse counted, but certain

---

[47]*Bible Numerics* (Philadelphia: Presbyterian and Reformed Publishing Co., 1961), p. 7.
[48]The full document can be seen in A. Cowley, *Aramaic Papyri of the Fifth Century B.C.* (Oxford: The Clarendon Press, 1923), p. 21 ff.

names and words are counted as they appear in the Bible as a whole. The lists usually include words such as "covenant, grace, holy, blood," and the names of "Jesus, Moses, and Paul." The idea behind this approach is that in Scripture all names, words, etc. that are really important will exhibit numeric patterns, usually with the number seven as its basis. Bullinger has this to say regarding this method:

> The actual number [of occurrences of certain words] depends upon the special significance of the word; for the significance of the word corresponds with the significance of the number of times it occurs. Where there is no special significance in the meaning or use of the word, there is no special significance in the number of its occurrences.[49]

This assumption, however, is open to serious question for it can be shown that not all important names or words occur in special numerical patterns. The name of Aaron appears 346 times in the Old Testament and 5 times in the New Testament for a total of 351 occurrences. None of these figures will provide us with a multiple of seven. Are we to assume that Aaron was therefore unimportant? The name of Moses, it is pointed out, occurs 847 times in the Bible (7 x 121). The number seven is usually associated with "completeness" or "perfection," and hence, the numerical pattern is appropriate as associated with Moses. If seven really carries this connotation however, how shall we interpret the fact that the name of the Canaanite god Baal occurs sixty-three times in the Bible (7 x 9)? Are we to assume that because the occurrences of this name total 63, a multiple of 7, that the name bears divine approval or perfection? On the other hand the name of Elijah only occurs 69 times in the Old Testament which is only six more than the pagan god Baal and is not a multiple of 7!

It should be obvious even to the casual observer that this system is purely speculative and not even consistent with itself.

Beside counting words, phrases, names and certain grammatical forms, the advocates of this theory devote considerable time establishing a "vocabulary" which is supposed to exhibit

---

[49]*Op. cit.,* pp. 22, 23. (brackets mine.)

numeric patterns. The "vocabulary" of a sentence is described by Panin:

> The form in which a word occurs is not necessarily the same as the vocabulary word. Thus "I struck him" has for its vocabulary "I, strike, he"; while the forms in which the words "strike" and "he" occur here are: "struck, him." A vocabulary of forms is thus hardly ever the same as the simple vocabulary.[50]

With devices like this, the numericist is able to extend his numerological patterns in all directions. Along with the establishment of "vocabulary" words, the various forms of these words are calculated also (e.g., nominative, genitive, accusative cases).

The real fallacies of this system of exegesis become evident when some of the methods of calculation are examined. In many parts of the Bible important passages of Scripture do not exhibit any observable numerical phenomena. When this occurs an appeal is made to "neighboring numbers." For example, in Panin's treatment of Genesis 1:1, he discovered that the "place value"[51] of the verse was only 298 and, therefore, not a multiple of either 7, 11, or 13. His treatment of this embarrassing problem is as follows:

> The bracketed item 298, though not a perfect multiple of either eleven or thirteen has been given to show a frequent phenomenon in Bible numerics: where now and then a number shows no numerics of itself, it is very likely within just one (and only one) of showing most striking numerics. So that though 298 is of itself no numeric number, it is within one of a multiple of both eleven and thirteen, by which numbers the schemes are already marked. That is to say: supposing a caviller should say to the Great Numberer, "How is this? Your 298 is neither a multiple of seven, not of eleven, not of thirteen. Do not numerics break down here?" The answer is:

---

[50]*Op. cit.,* XVII (1911), No. 1, p. 8, note 5.

[51]The place value of a letter is its place in the alphabet regardless of its numeric value. The letter *alpha* would therefore have the place value of 1, *beta*-2, *gamma*-3, etc. Omega has the numeric value of 800 but only 24 as place value (or should its place value be 26? The alphabet may have been larger in antiquity).

> Not so fast, Mr. Caviller, it is neither an eleven, nor a thir-
> teen, but it has both of them at each side; one at the right
> thereof, the other at the left thereof! . . . It is within one
> and only one, of a multiple of eleven, and within one, and only
> one, of a thirteen. The eleven and the thirteen thus stand
> guard at each side thereof, to protect it, as it were, from
> the slur that it shows no numerics after all![52]

Such reasoning hardly needs criticism, for it will fall under its
own weight. According to this argument a miss is not as good
as a mile or, in other words, a small miss is as good as a hit!
Such logic has no place in a serious consideration of Biblical
hermeneutics.

Gematria.[53] Gematria is that system of interpretation which
seeks to discover the hidden sense of the Hebrew and Greek
text through the numerical values of the letters of the alphabet.
William T. Smith defines this approach as follows:

> . . . the use of the letters of a word so as by means of
> their combined numerical value to express a name, or witty
> association of ideas.[54]

This whole system of exegesis operates upon the assumption that
the Greek and Hebrew alphabets always had numerical values
attached to them. It is at this point that the whole system
breaks down. It was demonstrated in Chapter 2 of this study
that the earliest traces of associating numerical values with the
letters of the alphabet belong to the Greeks of the sixth century
B.C. Evidence for the general use of this system among the
Jews in Palestine dates back only to about the third century
B.C. and its use seems to have been rather limited. It was the
conclusion of this writer that the idea of Gematria was an early
Greek innovation which was adopted by the Jews under Hellenistic influence.[55] The theological application of Gematria is
to be traced to the Talmudic, Midrashic, and Cabalastic liter-

---

[52]*Op. cit.,* XVII (Dec. 1911), No. 12, p. 141.
[53]*Gmtry'* a Hebraized form of *geōmetria.*
[54]*Op. cit.,* p. 2162.
[55]See page 126 ff. for full discussion.

atures of the Jews. The Gnostics were also responsible for detailed application and expansion to theological truths. In the more recent books and articles on numerics employing Gematria, mention is never made of its origin or development. The reader is always given the impression that (1) the Greek and Hebrew alphabets always had numerical values associated with them, (2) what is presented is in effect a "new discovery,"[56] and (3) that numbers have always had symbolical or theological values.

It is usually the goal of numericists to try to find as many numerical "features" as possible in a given verse. The "features" that are usually presented are indeed impressive as Panin's treatment of Gensis 1:1 demonstrates:

> The numeric value of the first word of this verse is 913; of the last 296; of the middle, the fourth word, 401; the numeric value of the first, middle and last words is thus 1610, or 230 sevens (Feature 7); the numeric value of the first, middle, and last letters of the 28 letters of this verse is 133, or 19 sevens (Feature 8). If now the first and last letters of each of the seven words in this verse have their numeric value placed against them, we have for their numeric value 1383, or 199 sevens (Feature 9), etc.[57]

In this verse Panin was able to find twenty-five "features" involving sevens which, of course, was considered proof of its inspiration. More recent analysis of Genesis 1:1 has provided us with symmetries and factor runs.[58] What is really interesting about these various numerical analyses is not what is pointed out, but what is omitted. The following is the Hebrew text of Genesis 1:1 with the accompanying numerical values:

A careful analysis of this verse provides us with the following phenomena. The total for the seven words in the verse is

---

[56]Cf. the discussion of Sabiers' work on p. 134 f.

[57]Ivan Panin, op. cit., XVII (Dec. 1911), No. 12, p. 140.

[58]D. David Smith, Gematria and New Masorah of Genesis 1:1 (Minneapolis, Minn: Micro-text, 1963).

2701. This is not a multiple of 7 but is one less ($2702 = 7 \times 386$), (Feature 1).[59] Only one word out of the seven in the verse has a numeric value involving a multiple of 7. That word is "Created" (*br'*) which totals 203 (7 x 29), (Feature 2). The word "God" (*'lhym*) does not even provide a multiple of 7. Its total numerical value is 86 (2 x 43). According to the symbolical implications of this total (i.e., not being a multiple 7), the name must be regarded as unimportant (Feature 3). The total value of the first and last letter of the verse is 92 and this is not a multiple of 7 although it only misses it by 1 ($91 = 7$ x 13), (Feature 4). The letter *aleṗ* only occurs six times in the verse and not 7. Its total numerical value is likewise only 6 (Feature 5). The two direct object signs (*'t*) of the verse add up to 802 which is not a multiple of 7 (Feature 6). The two direct objects have as their numeric totals 395 (*hšmym*) and 296 (*h'rṣ*). The total of these two numbers is 691 which is not a multiple of 7 (Feature 7).

It will not serve the purpose of this argument to continue "feature" hunting in this verse for it is quite clear that one can easily find mathematical data which in no way exhibits the magical seven. If the inspiration of a verse or chapter of the Bible depended on its mathematical structure, most of our Bible would have to be abandoned as uninspired.

There are two texts, however, which seem to exhibit Gematria and these are usually cited as proof of the fact that this system was not only known to the scribes, but that they actually employed the system. One text is Genesis 14:14, which indicates that Abraham had 318 servants. An analysis of the name Eliezer (*'ly'zr*, Gen. 15:2), a servant of Abraham, reveals that it has a numerical value of 318. Regarding this data Dantzig argues as follows:

> Not only was Gematria used from the earliest days for the interpretation of Biblical passages, but there are indications that the writers of the Bible had practiced the art. Thus Abraham proceeding to the rescue of his brother Eliasar (sic!) drives

---

[59]The total is, of course, a "neighbor" to a multiple of seven, but since it is not exactly seven, the verse therefore, must be considered of less value, perhaps, than a verse with an exact multiple of seven!

forth 318 slaves. Is it just a coincidence that the Hebrew word
Eliasar adds up to 318?[60]

The answer to the question Dantzig raises is, yes. It is just
coincidental that the name Eliezer has a numeric value of 318,
which was the number of Abraham's servants. With a little
imagination one can easily discover data such as this. In fact,
the possibilities of discovering the novel in Scripture are limit-
less. Note, for example, that the apocryphal Epistle of Barnabas
(9:8) interpreted the number 318 as a reference to the crucified
Christ because the 300 in Greek was designated by the letter
which formed a cross and the 18 by *iota, eta,* the abbreviation
of *Iēsous.* This view was also proposed by Clement of Alexan-
dria.[61] The "three men which stood by him" in Genesis 18:2
could be identified even though their names do not appear in
the text according to the Jewish numericist. He discovered that
the phrase "lo three men stood by him" had a numerical value
of 701, the same value as "these are Michael, Gabriel and
Raphael." (*'lw myk'l gbry'l wrp'l*). His conclusion, therefore,
was that the three men not named in Genesis 18 were these
angels.

The initial and final letters of several words were sometimes
formed into separate words thus providing new ideas. For example letters from the beginnings and ends of the words *my
y'lh lnw hsmymh* "who shall go up for us to heaven?" (Deut.
30:12) are placed together to form *mylh* "circumcision" (initial
letters) and *yhwh* "Yahweh" (final letters). It was inferred
from this combination that God ordained circumcision as the way
to heaven.[62]

Since the phrase *yb' sylh* (Gen. 49:10) had a numerical value
of 358 it was argued that this was a Messianic prophecy because *mšyḥ*, "Messiah" also had a numerical value of 358.

The other text which has received the most attention be-

---

[60]*Op. cit.,* p. 39.

[61]*The Stromata,* Book VI, Chap. XI, Alexander and Donaldson, *op. cit.,*
II, p. 499.

[62]Cf. Christian D. Ginsburg, *The Essenes, The Kabbala* (New York: The
Macmillan Co., 1956), p. 132.

cause it appeared to exhibit Gematria is Revelation 13:18 which reads:

> Here is wisdom. Let him that hath understanding count the number of the beast: for it is the number of a man; and his number is six hundred three score and six (KJV).

Some texts represent the number 666 by the letters *chi xi sigma*. This, according to some, is the final proof of the fact that Gematria was used by Bible writers. In answer to this assertion it should be pointed out that not all texts contain this reading. Some manuscripts have the number written out and some contain the variant reading 616 instead of 666.[63] Even if the original reading was *chi xi sigma* it cannot be proved that the number *per se* contained mystical or symbolical values. One only has to view the multitude of attempts to identify the Anti-christ on the basis of this number to see the futility of exegesis based on Gematria.

In antiquity Nero was considered a likely candidate for Antichrist because his name, when written with Hebrew characters, had a numerical value of 666. The numerical analysis of his name is as follows:

$$
\begin{array}{rl}
\text{ן} =& 50 \\
\text{ר} =& 200 \\
\text{ו} =& 6 \\
\text{ן} =& 50 \\
\text{כ} =& 100 \\
\text{ס} =& 60 \\
\text{ר} =& 200 \\
\hline
& 666
\end{array}
$$

Irenaeus, in *Against Heresies*, makes mention of the fact that the term *lateinos* was a possible identification because it had a numerical value of 666, although he does not seem to adopt the idea. The values of the letters are as follows: *lambda* = 30, *alpha* = 1, *tau* = 300, *epsilon* = 5, *iota* = 10, *nu* = 50,

---

[63]The reading of 666, however, does seem to be the preferred reading. See Gerhard Kittel, ed., *Theological Dictionary of the New Testament* (Grand Rapids: Wm. B. Eerdmans Publishing Co., 1964), I, p. 463.

omicron = 70, *sigma* = 200.[64] His comment on this number is interesting and instructive:

> It is therefore more certain, and less hazardous, to await the fulfillment of the prophecy, than to be making surmises, and casting about for any names that may present themselves, insomuch as many names can be found possessing the number.[65]

Henry Alford feels that the word *lateinos* comes the closest to the solution of the problem although he too prefers to leave the matter open to question.[66] Other candidates include Pope Leo X,[67] Martin Luther, [68] and Trajan Hadrianus. Some explanations of the number are based on the form of the number 666 as it appears in the text. In *Things to Come*, the following solution was offered:

> . . . the great significance of this number is seen when we remember that the secret symbol of the great ancient pagan mysteries was SSS or 666; and that today it is the connecting link between them and their revival in Spiritism and Theosophy which aim at the union of all religions into one.

> The first and last of these three letters are the abbreviation of the word, *Christos*. So that, when we have the Ɛ , like a crooked serpent, put between them, we see a fitting symbol of Satan's Messiah — Anti-Christ.[69]

The most artificial solution found by this writer was that of Frederick Dunning in *The Christian Century*.[70] His discussion is as follows:

---

[64]*Against Heresies*, Book V, chap. 30, Alexander & Donaldson, *op. cit.*, I, p. 559.

[65]*Ibid.*

[66]*Op. cit.*, IV, p. 683.

[67]Proposed by Michael Stifel, a German algebraist of the sixteenth century, see E. T. Bell, *op. cit.*, p. 169.

[68]Proposed by Peter Bung, a sixteenth century encyclopedist of numerology, E. T. Bell, *Ibid.*

[69]*Things to Come*, X (July 1903), No. 2, p. 12.

[70]"Ku Klux Fulfills the Scripture," *The Christian Century*, XLI (Sept. 18, 1924), No. 38.

This riddle has puzzled the minds of Bible students for centuries, but when the Ku Klux Klan is used as the key, it
becomes as simple as child's play. Let us start with the magic
letters K.K.K. with their proper punctuation marks. Webster tells us that "multiplicaton is often expressed by a dot between the factors," thus K.K.K. = K x K x K. The numerical
value of K is eleven, as it is the eleventh letter in both the
English and Hebrew alphabets. Substituting this value for K
we have K.K.K. = 11 x 11 x 11 = 1331. This is the sample
numerical value of K.K.K. But there is one lacking. The
founder and first head of the K.K.K. has been cast out and
must be restored before we have the perfect symbol of the
Ku Klux Klan. Adding the lost one in we have 1331 plus 1 =
1332. This is the perfect numerical value of the Ku Klux Klan.
The number in verse 18, however, is the number of the beast
while in the chapter as a whole the Ku Klux Klan is represented
by two beasts, namely, the beast with seven heads and ten
horns representing the dynasty of William Joseph, King of Ku,
and the beast that looked like a lamb but "spake as a dragon"
representing the dynasty of Hiram, King of Klux. Therefore,
to get the number of one beast we must divide the complete
number by two (1332 ÷ 2 = 666). And this is the number
by which the prophet may be known. . . .[71]

Such superficial exegesis is characteristic of those who indulge
in mystical numerology.[72] Numbers are assigned to the letters
in some suitably chosen or invented alphabet, the letters of the
intended victim's name are given their numbers, and these are
added. If the sum does not come out to the desired 666, the
name is appropriately mispelled and if necessary, more than one
alphabet is employed. Sometimes, when the numericist is un-
able to attach a meaning to a name in its native language, the
name is spelled in a foreign language. If this fails, plain jargon
is used. It should be obvious that such exegetical methodology
has no place in a sound system of hermeneutics. Any sort of
identification for the Anti-christ is possible if one tries hard

---

[71]*Ibid.*, p. 1207.
[72]For an association of the number 666 with Germany and the Kaiser
see J. Bernard Nicklin, *Signposts of History* (Merrimac, Mass.: Destiny
Publishers, 1956), p. 23 f.

enough. I recalled noting the fact that I was born in 1936. When factors of 36 are totaled,[73] we have 666! This discovery was made in room 36 in a hotel in Chicago on July 6 (exactly 36 days from June 1)! The implications of these numbers are staggering![74]

The Holy Spirit did not see fit to identify the Anti-christ in Revelation 13:18, which may be an indication that his name is not for us to know. This perhaps explains the use of the mysterious number 666. In fact, if II Thessalonians 2:7, 8 has reference to the Rapture of the Church, no one will know who the Anti-christ really is until the Tribulation period.

One other text which has caught the imagination of commentators is John 21:11. At least eighteen different interpretations have been offered for the meaning or significance of this number.[75] Many have felt that since the exact number of fishes is given in the text, it must bear some special significance.

> St. Jerome makes reference to a zoologist subsequent to John (whom, however, we now know, he misread) according to whom there are 153 species of fish. Thus the purpose of the text is to declare that in the church (= the net), without losing its unity, there is room for all the races of mankind.[76]

Augustine proposed a similar view based on the fact that the sum of the factor of 17 equalled 153. His conclusion was that:

> All, therefore, who are sharers in such grace are symbolized by this number, that is, are symbolically represented.[77]

A more speculative proposal is presented by P. H. Menound.

> P. H. Menound has communicated the following interpretation to me, and it seems to me very attractive: it is necessary, he

---

[73]i.e., $1 + 2 + 3 + 4 + 5 \ldots + 34 + 35 + 36 = 666$.

[74]I do, however, find comfort in the fact that my full name, John James Davis, has 14 letters in it (2×7)!

[75]J. A. Emerton, "The Hundred and Fifty-three Fishes in John 21:11," *The Journal of Theological Studies*, IX (April, 1958), p. 87.

[76]J. J. von Allmen, "Numbers," *A Companion to the Bible* (New York: Oxford University Press, 1958), p. 311.

[77]*On the Gospel of John*, Schaff, *op. cit.*, VI, pp. 442, 443.

says, to join the net to the fish, that is to say, add 1 and 17. In this way the number 18 is obtained, the equivalent in alphabetical transposition of the first two letters, in Greek, of the name Jesus (I H). . . . The sense, then, would be as follows: the preaching of Jesus (= the casting of the net) and the believers which it gathers in, in other words the church, appear in the world as the same saving power as Jesus was during the time of His incarnation.[78]

The list of such speculations is an endless one and still growing. Such interpretations are purely artificial and arbitrary and have no place in a Christian theology. Without further discussion of such proposals let us evaluate the whole system of mystical numbers as a hermeneutical principle.

D. Evaluation of This System

After a careful analysis of the claims and the methods proposed by the advocates of Bible numerics, it is our conclusion that the whole system must be rejected as a valid method of exegesis. The following are the reasons for this conclusion: (1) This system is based on a false apologetic, namely, if wonderful numerical pattern can be established, the world will no longer be able to reject the Bible as uninspired. It is claimed that there is numeric precision in nature so there must be in the Word of God. But we should like to ask, what is all this to a blind man? What man has ever beheld the holiness of Christ in the numeric patterns of nature and was saved? If human depravity is all that the Scriptures describe it to be, no amount of numeric evidence will rationalize the sinner into salvation. Only the Spirit of God can make an individual aware of his condition before God.

(2) This phenomenon can be applied to any numbers. Allis has illustrated this point well with the number 1776, the year of the Declaration of Independence. It has two 7's in it. Add the first and last number together and you have another 7, etc.[79]

(3) There is no objective basis for controlling this methodology. The interpreter selects his words, and the combinations of

---

[78]J. J. von Allmen, *loc. cit.*, p. 311.
[79]See Allis, *op. cit.*, pp. 3, 4 for a complete illustration of this point. Also cf. p. 24.

numbers that he wishes. In other words 7 might have several combinations (6+ 1, 5 + 2, 4 + 3). How do we know which of these combinations the author intended to bear symbolic implications?

(4) The appeal to "neighboring numbers" is not only a mathematical absurdity, but renders the symbolism of numbers meaningless.

(5) This whole system is based on a false premise. There is no proof that the Hebrews of the Old Testament used their alphabet in this manner (i.e., in Gematria). As was pointed out earlier, the Moabite Stone and the Siloam Inscription have their numbers written out. This is the case in all the Old Testament. If we should grant that the Hebrews did use their alphabet in this manner, it has yet to be proven that these two factors (i.e., Gematria and Number Symbolism) are combined in Scripture.

(6) This system of interpretation contributes nothing to a better understanding of the text. If anything, it complicates the simplicity of the Word of God. Any method of interpretation which operates on subjective notions is a scheme, not a system, and has no real place in the methods of hermeneutics.

PART III

SUMMARY AND CONCLUSIONS

Chapter 7

SUMMARY AND CONCLUSIONS

The aims of this study were threefold: (1) to collect, analyze and classify data relevant to numbers and their use in the Bible, (2) to define the nature and use of numbers in Scripture, and (3) by experimentation and evaluation to establish valid and consistent principles for the interpretation of Biblical numbers.

The first section of this work dealt with the construction of numbers in the Bible and in contemporary literature. It was shown that in the Bible numbers are always written out as full words, but in other inscriptional materials contemporary with the Bible a number of systems of numeral notation were employed. The Bible nowhere exhibits the use of the alphabet for numerical values.[1] The employment of the alphabet for numeral notations seems to have been a rather late innovation (fourth–third centuries B.C.). The idea of using the alphabet for numerical notation appears to be of Greek origin.

The second major section of this study dealt with the four basic uses of numbers in the Bible. The first and most common use of numbers in the Bible was noted to be the conventional use found in a variety of contexts. The employment of numbers in this manner is intended to denote either a specific or a general mathematical quantity. It was noted that the Old Testament does not display a great quantity of mathematical processes, but that which is in evidence is accurate and indicative of the work of a careful scribe. Conventional numbers present a number of problems of interpretation especially when they are very large numbers. The problems connected with the size of the exodus, large military census, and population statistics were considered and it was concluded that there was no reason why these numbers, even though large, should not be regarded as actual and dependable. Rejection of large numbers in the Old Testament was usually characteristic of the liberal-critical position, not because of statistical impossibility, but because in many

---

[1]With the possible exception of Rev. 13:18.

cases it involved miracles which critics, *a priori*, dismiss as impossible. There were a number of texts employing numbers conventionally which exhibited apparent corruptions. These texts were few in number and in most cases could be adjusted on the basis of other texts or archaeological evidence.

Rhetorical numbers form a very important class of numbers in the Bible. An expression employing numbers for rhetorical effect does not attempt to emphasize the mathematical value of the number, but concepts such as "few," "many," etc. The climactic use of numbers, expressed by the formula $x/x+1$, was found to be very common in the Old Testament. Significant parallels to this usage were found in Ugaritic and Akkadian literature. It was noted that the $x/x+1$ formula was employed most frequently in the poetic portions of the Old Testament. This formula could be used in three ways: (1) As a poetic device to intensify the meaning of a phrase, (2) as a mathematical expression having actual numerical value, and (3) as an indefinite value conveying the ideas of a "few" or "many."

The third class of numbers in the Old Testament was the symbolic number. After careful examination of the data of the Old Testament and the historical development of symbolic numbers in extra-biblical literature, it was the conclusion of this writer that the Bible does not use numbers symbolically to convey theological truths. The only number which seemed to be clearly used symbolically was the number seven and then only to convey the general idea of "fullness" or "completion." This idea, in connection with the number seven, was shown to be a common literary phenomenon in contemporary non-biblical inscriptions. The exegetical method of ascribing theological values to numbers was demonstrated to be of Greek origin and that it found its development primarily among the Gnostics, Neo-Pythagoreans and Jewish allegorists. The Christianization of this system was concluded to have been a Post-Apostolic development pursued mainly by the Church Fathers.

The last use of numbers examined in this general section was the mystical use of numbers. Mystical numbers are supposed to carry hidden meanings or theological concepts. A careful examination of this whole system was undertaken and the historical precedents for this type of hermeneutic were analyzed and it was concluded that the Bible does not use numbers in a mystical sense. There is no evidence that the letters of the alphabet were used to convey numerical values along with theological concepts. The theory of mystical numbers was demonstrated to be of Greek origin and its success or failure as a system of interpretation depended largely on the imagination of the interpreter rather than objective evidence. When numbers and/or letters of the alphabet are given mystical or theological values, there is no end to speculations which might follow. Good examples of the extravagant claims which interpreters might make using Gematria or similar devices are found in the modern works of Bullinger and Sabiers.[2] Mystical numerology has also been an integral part of the theory of Pyramidologists.[3] It was the conclusion of this writer that this system of interpretation has no place in the historical-grammatical interpretation of Scripture.

Conclusion

It is the conclusion of this writer that with reference to the interpretation of the numbers of the Bible that the following rules be followed: (1) Numbers should always be taken at face value and understood as conveying a mathematical quantity unless there is either textual or contextual evidence to the contrary.[4] (2) When the numerical sequence $x/x+1$ occurs in a synonymous, synthetic or antithetic parallelism it is most likely intended to intensify the idea of the parallelism. The mathematical values of the formula, in most cases, is not of significance. The $x/x+1$ formula may also be employed to denote a concept such as "few." (3) The number seven should be regarded as a

---

[2] See page 133ff.

[3] For a presentation of the system of Pyramidology see:

Joseph A. Seiss, *A Miracle in Stone* (Philadelphia: Porter & Coates, n.d.).

George R. Riffert, *Great Pyramid, Proof of God* (Merrimac, Mass: Destiny Publishers, 1960).

J. Bernard Nicklin, *Testimony in Stone* (Merrimac, Mass: Destiny Publishers, 1961).

A refutation of this system of exegesis may be found in: Wilbur M. Smith, *Egypt in Biblical Prophecy* (Boston: W. A. Wilde Company, 1957).

[4] Cf. Gerald T. Kennedy, *op. cit.*, p. 34.

literal mathematical value unless the context, by obvious repeti-
tion of the number, or specific reference indicates that the number conveys the additional idea of "complete." (4) All numbers
of the Bible should be regarded as fundamentally dependable
and the interpreter should be hesitant to change the traditional
text unless there is clear evidence of textual corruption and only
when he has sufficient evidence to support the new reading.

BIBLIOGRAPHY

Books

Albright, William. *Archaeology and the Religion of Israel.* Baltimore: The Johns Hopkins Press, 1953.

—————. *From the Stone Age to Christianity.* Baltimore: The Johns Hopkins Press, 1957.

—————. *The Archaeology of Palestine.* Baltimore: Penguin Books, 1961.

—————. *The Biblical Period.* Pittsburgh: 1955.

Alexander, Joseph A. *The Psalms Translated and Explained.* Grand Rapids: Zondervan Publishing House, n.d.

Alford, L. A. *Mystic Numbers of the Word.* Logansport, Ind.: L. A. Alford & Son, 1870.

Allis, Oswald T. *Bible Numerics.* Philadelphia: Presbyterian and Reformed Publishing Co., 1961.

Archer, Gleason L. *A Survey of Old Testament Introduction.* Chicago: Moody Press, 1964.

Baillet, M., Milik, J. T., and de Vaux, Roland. *Discoveries in the Judean Desert of Jordan III, Texts.* Oxford: The Clarendon Press, 1962.

Baramki, Dimitri. *Phoenicia and the Phoenicians.* Beirut: Khayats, 1961.

Barr, James. *The Semantics of Biblical Language.* Glasgow: The University Press, 1961.

Barton, George A. *Archaeology and the Bible.* Philadelphia: American Sunday School Union, 1916.

Bauer, Theo. *Akkadische Lesestücke.* Roma: Pontificium Institutum Biblicum, 1953 (Heft I-III).

Begley, Walter. *Biblia Cabalistica.* London: David Nutt, 1903.

Bell, E. T. *Numerology, The Magic of Numbers.* New York: United Book Guild, 1945.

—————. *Numerology.* New York: The Century Co., 1933.

Bennett, W. H. *The Moabite Stone.* Edinburgh: T. & T. Clark, 1911.

Brown, Francis; Driver, S. R.; Briggs, Charles A. *A Hebrew and English Lexicon of the Old Testament.* Oxford: The Clarendon Press, 1952.

Bruce, F. F. *The Books and The Parchments.* Westwood, N. J.: Fleming H. Revell Co., 1963 (Revised).

Budge, E. A. Wallis. *Easy Lessons in Egyptian Hieroglyphics.* London: Kegan Paul, Trench, Trubner & Co., Ltd., 1899.

——————. *First Steps in Egyptian.* London: Kegan Paul, Trench, Trubner & Co., 1895.

Bullinger, E. W. *How to Enjoy the Bible.* London: The Lamp Press, 1955.

——————. *Number in Scripture.* London: Eyre & Spottiswoode Ltd., 1913; reprinted 1967, by Kregel Publications, Grand Rapids.

Burrows, Millar. *More Light on the Dead Sea Scrolls.* New York: The Viking Press, 1958.

Buttmann, Alexander. *A Grammar of the New Testament Greek.* Andover: Warren F. Draper, 1880.

Buttrick, George Arthur (ed.). *The Interpreter's Dictionary of the Bible.* New York: Abingdon Press, 1962.

Cheiro, Louis H. *Cheiro's Book of Numbers.* New York: Garden City Publishing Company, Inc., 1912.

Clarke, John C. C. *The Origin and Varieties of the Semitic Alphabet.* Chicago: The American Publication Society of Hebrew, 1884.

Cohen, A. (ed.). *The Soncino Books of the Bible.* London: The Soncino Press, 1951.

Conart, Levi Leonard. *The Number Concept.* New York: Macmillan and Co., 1923.

Cooke, G. A. *A Text-Book of North-Semitic Inscriptions.* Oxford: The Clarendon Press, 1903.

Cowley, A. *Aramaic Papyri of the Fifth Century B.C.* Oxford: The Clarendon Press, 1923.

Dantzig, Tobias. *Number, The Language of Science.* New York: The Macmillan Company, 1959.

——————. *The Bequest of the Greeks.* New York: Charles Scribner's Sons, 1955.

Davidson, A. B. *The Theology of the Old Testament.* New York: Charles Scribner's Sons, 1907.

Davidson, F. *The New Bible Commentary.* Grand Rapids: Wm. B. Eerdmans Publishing Co., 1963.

Davis, John D. *A Dictionary of the Bible.* Grand Rapids: Baker Book House, 1954.

de Vaux, Roland. *Ancient Israel, Its Life and Institutions.* Trans. John McHugh. London: Darton, Longman and Todd, 1961.

Diringer, David. *The Alphabet.* New York: Philosophical Library, 1948.

Donner, H. and Rollig, W. *Kanaanaische und Aramaische Inschriften.* Wiesbaden: Otto Harrassowitz, 1962.

Douglas, J. D. (ed.). *The New Bible Dictionary.* Grand Rapids: Wm. B. Eerdmans Publishing Co., 1962.

Driver, G. R. *Aramaic Documents of the 5th Century B.C.* Oxford: The Clarendon Press, 1957.

Driver, S. R. *Notes on the Hebrew Text and the Topography of the Books of Samuel.* Oxford: The Clarendon Press, 1913.

----------. *The Book of Exodus.* Cambridge: The University Press, 1953.

Edersheim, Alfred. *The Life and Times of Jesus the Messiah.* New York: Longmans, Green and Co., 1904. Vol. I & II.

Ferm, Vergilius. *An Encyclopedia of Religion.* New York: The Philosophical Libarary, 1945.

Finegan, Jack. *Handbook of Biblical Chronology.* Princeton: Princeton University Press, 1964.

----------. *Light From the Ancient Past.* Princeton: Princeton University Press, 1959.

Franken, H. J. and Battershill, C. A. *A Primer of Old Testament Archaeology.* Leiden: E. J. Brill, 1963.

Gelb, I. J. *A Study of Writing.* Chicago: The University of Chicago Press, 1952.

----------. *Morphology of Akkadian.* Chicago: by the author, 1952.

Ghyka, Matila. *Philosophie et Mystique du Nombre.* Paris: Payot, 1952.

Ginsburg, Christian D. *The Essenes, The Kabbala.* New York: Macmillan Co., 1956.

Goldman, S. "Samuel," *The Soncino Books of the Bible.* A. Cohen, ed., London: The Soncino Press, 1951.

Goodenough, Erwin R. *By Light, Light, The Mystic Gospel of Hellenistic Judaism.* New Haven: Yale University Press, 1935.

Gordon, Cyrus H. *Introduction to Old Testament Times.* Ventnor: Ventnor Publishers, Inc., 1953.

----------. *Ugaritic Literature.* Rome: Pontifical Bible Institute. 1949.

----------. *The World of the Old Testament.* New York: Doubleday & Company, Inc., 1958.

Gray, George B. *A Critical and Exegetical Commentary on Numbers.* New York: Charles Scribner's Sons, 1920.

Gray, James C. and Adams, George M. *Bible Commentary.* Vol. I Grand Rapids: Zondervan Publishing House, n.d.

Green, Samuel G. *Handbook to the Grammar of the Greek Testament.* New York: Fleming H. Revell Co., 1912.

Greene, John. *The Hebrew Migration From Egypt.* London: Trubner and Co., 1879.

Hartill, J. Edwin. *Biblical Hermeneutics*. Grand Rapids: Zondervan Publishing House, 1960.

Hastings, James (ed.). *Dictionary of the Apostolic Church*. New York: Charles Scribner's Sons, 1918.

Hebert, A. G. *The Authority of the Old Testament*. London: Faber and Faber Ltd., 1947.

Heinisch, Paul. *Theology of the Old Testament*. St. Paul: The North Central Publishing Co., 1955.

Hogben, Lancelot. *Mathematics in the Making*. Garden City: Doubleday and Company, 1960.

Hopper, Vincent. *Medieval Number Symbolism*. New York: Columbia University Press, 1938.

Jackson, Samuel M. (ed.). *The New Schaff-Herzog Encyclopedia of Religious Knowledge*. Grand Rapids: Baker Book House, 1950.

Jacob, Edmond. *Theology of the Old Testament*. New York: Harper & Brothers Publishers, 1958.

Karpinski, Louis C. *The History of Arithmetic*. Chicago: Rand McNally & Co., 1925.

Kasner, Edward and Newman, James. *Mathematics and the Imagination*. New York: Simon and Schuster, 1952.

Keil, C. F. and Delitzsch, F. *Biblical Commentary on the Old Testament*. Grand Rapids: Wm. B. Eerdmans Publishing Co., 1950.

Keyser, Cassius J. *Science and Religion, The Rational and the Superrational*. New Haven: Yale University Press, 1914.

Kinney, LeBaron W. *The Greatest Thing in the Universe*. New York: Loizeaux Brothers, 1939.

Kittel, Gerhard (Ed.). *Theological Dictionary of the New Testament*. Grand Rapids: Wm. B. Eerdmans Publishing Co., 1964.

Knudson, Albert C. *The Religious Teaching of the Old Testament*. New York: Abingdon Cokesbury Press, 1960.

Koehler, Ludwig and Baumgartner, Walter (eds.). *Lexicon in Veteris Testamenti Libros*. Leiden: E. J. Brill, 1958.

Kozminsky, Isidore. *Numbers, Their Meaning and Magic*. New York: G. P. Putnam's Sons, 1927.

Kramer, Samuel. *The Sumerians*. Chicago: The University of Chicago Press, 1963.

Lange, John P. *Commentary on the Holy Scriptures*. Trans. by Philip Schaff. Grand Rapids: Zondervan Publishing House, 1915.

Lea, Thomas Simcox and Bond, Frederick Bligh. *Materials for the Study of the Apostolic Gnosis*. Boston: Marshall Jones Co., 1920.

Lenski, R. C. H. *The Interpretation of the Acts of the Apostles.* Columbus, Ohio: The Wartburg Press, 1944.

Leupold, H. C. *Exposition of Genesis.* Grand Rapids: Baker Book House, 1941.

Mahan, M. *Palmoni or The Numerals of Scripture.* New York: D. Appleton and Company, 1863.

Maziarz, Edward A. *The Philosophy of Mathematics.* New York: Philosophical Library, 1950.

McCormack, R. *Seven in Scripture.* London: Marshall Brothers, Limited, 1926.

McIntosh, C. H. *Notes on the Book of Numbers.* New York: M. Cathcart, 1869.

Mendenhall, George E. *Law and Covenant in Israel and the Ancient Near East.* Pittsburgh: The Biblical Colloquium, 1955.

Michell, George. *The Historical Truth of the Bible.* London: Marshall Brothers, Limited, 1926.

Mickelsen, A. Berkeley. *Interpreting the Bible.* Grand Rapids: Wm. B. Eerdmans Publishing Co., 1963.

Mordell, Phineas. *The Origin of Letters and Numerals.* Philadelphia: Phineas Mordell, 1914.

Morton, A. Q. and McLeman, James. *Christianity in the Computer Age.* New York: Harper and Row, 1964.

Moulton, James H. *A Grammar of New Testament Greek.* Edinburgh: T. & T. Clark, 1957. 3 Vols.

Nesbit, William. *Sumerian Records from Drehem.* New York: Columbia University Press, 1914.

Neugebauer, O. *The Exact Sciences in Antiquity.* New York: Harper and Brothers, 1957.

Nichol, Francis D. (ed.). *The Seventh-day Adventist Bible Commentary.* Washington, D.C.: Review and Herald Publishing Association, 1953.

Nicklin, J. Bernard. *Signposts of History.* Merrimac, Mass.: Destiny Publishers, 1956.

Noth, Martin. *The History of Israel.* New York: Harper and Row, Publishers, 1960.

Oehler, Gustave F. *Theology of the Old Testament.* Grand Rapids: Zondervan Publishing House, n.d.

Orr, James (ed.). *The International Standard Bible Encyclopaedia.* Chicago: The Howard-Severance Co., 1925.

Payne, J. Barton. *The Theology of the Older Testament*. Grand
    Rapids: Zondervan Publishing House, 1962.
Petrie, W. M. Flinders. *Researches in Sinai*. London: Hazell, Wat-
    son and Viney, Ltd., 1906.
Pfeiffer, Charles F. *Ras Shamra and the Bible*. Grand Rapids:
    Baker Book House, 1962.
Pfeiffer, Charles F. and Harrison, Everett F. (eds.) *The Wycliffe
    Bible Commentary*. Chicago: Moody Press, 1963.
Pierson, Arthur. *Knowing The Scriptures*. New York: Gospel Pub-
    lishing House, 1910.
Pinches, Theophilus G. *An Outline of Assyrian Grammar*. London:
    Henry J. Glaisher, 1910.
Pritchard, James B. (ed.) *Ancient Near Eastern Texts*. Princeton:
    Princeton University Press, 1955.

Ramm, Bernard. *The Christian View of Science and Scripture*.
    Grand Rapids: Wm. B. Eerdmans Publishing Co., 1954.
----------. *Protestant Biblical Interpretation*. Boston: W. A. Wilde
    Company, 1956.
Roberts, Alexander and Donaldson, James (eds.). *The Ante-Nicene
    Fathers*. Grand Rapids: Wm. B. Eerdmans Publishing Company,
    1950. 9 Vols.
Robertson, A. T. *A Grammar of the Greek New Testament in the
    Light of Historical Research*. New York: Hodder and Stroughton,
    1915.
Rosenthal, Franz. *A Grammar of Biblical Aramaic*. Wiesbaden: Otto
    Harrassowitz, 1961.
Rowley, H. H. *From Joseph to Joshua*. London: Oxford University
    Press, 1958.
----------. *The Rediscovery of the Old Testament*. Philadelphia: The
    Westminster Press, 1946.
Russell, D. S. *The Method and Message of Jewish Apocalyptic*.
    Philadelphia: The Westminster Press, 1964.
Rutherford, Adam. *Treatise on Bible Chronology*. London: The
    Institute of Pyramidology, 1957.

Sabiers, M. A. *Astounding New Discoveries*. Los Angeles: Robertson
    Publishing Co., 1941.
Schaff, Philip (ed.). *A Select Library of the Nicene and Post-Nicene
    Fathers of the Christian Church*. Buffalo: The Christian Litera-
    ture Co., 1886. 14 Vols.
Schultz, Hermann. *Old Testament Theology*. Edinburgh: T. Clark,
    1892.

Seiss, Joseph A. *A Miracle in Stone.* Philadelphia: The United Lutheran Publication House, 1877.

Slotki, Israel W. *The Talmud Erubin.* London: The Soncino Press, 1938.

Slotki, Judah J. (tr.). *Midrash Rabbah, Numbers.* London: The Soncino Press, 1939.

Smeltzer, Donald. *Man and Number.* New York: Emerson Books, Inc.

Smith, D. David. *Gematria and New Masorah of Genesis 1:1.* Minneapolis, Minn: Micro-Text, 1963.

Smith, H. P. *The Books of Samuel, The International Critical Commentary.* New York: Charles Scribner's Sons, 1909.

Smith, Henry P. *Essays in Biblical Interpretation.* Boston: Marshall Jones Company, 1921.

Springer, J. Arthur. *Practical Christian Living.* Chicago: Moody Press, 1951.

Steinmueller, John E. and Sullivan, Kathryn. *Catholic Biblical Encyclopedia, Old Testament.* New York City: Joseph F. Wagner, 1959.

Terry, Milton S. *Biblical Hermeneutics.* Grand Rapids: Zondervan Publishing House, n.d.

Thayer, Alexander W. *The Hebrews and the Red Sea.* Andover: Warren F. Draper, 1883.

Thayer, Joseph H. *Greek-English Lexicon of the New Testament.* New York: Harper and Brothers, 1889.

Thomson, William M. *The Land and The Book.* New York: Harper and Brothers, 1908. 3 Vols.

Tuck, Robert. *A Handbook of Biblical Difficulties.* New York: Fleming H. Revell Company, 1914.

Unger, Merrill F. *Archaeology and the Old Testament.* Grand Rapids: Zondervan Publishing House, 1954.

_____ (ed.). *Unger's Bible Dictionary.* Chicago: Moody Press, 1957.

Ventris, Michael and Chadwick, John. *Documents in Mycenaean Greek.* Cambridge: The University Press, 1956.

Von Allmen, Jean-Jacques (ed.). *Vocabulaire Biblique.* Paris: Delachaux and Nestle, 1954.

Webster, Noah and McKechnie, Jean L. (eds.). *Webster's New Twentieth Century Dictionary of the English Language.* Unabridged. New York: The World Publishing Co., 1963.

Wedberg, Anders. *Plato's Philosophy of Mathematics.* Stockholm: Almquist and Wiksell, 1955.

Welch, Charles H. *An Alphabetical Analysis of Terms and Texts Used in the Study of Dispensational Truth.* Surry, England: The Berean Publishing Trust, 1958.

Whitcomb, John C. and Morris, Henry M. *The Genesis Flood.* Philadelphia: The Presbyterian and Reformed Publishing Co., 1961.

Wood, James D. *The Interpretation of the Bible.* London: Gerald Duckworth and Co. Ltd., 1958.

Woodhead, A. G. *The Study of Greek Inscriptions.* Cambridge: The University Press, 1959.

Wright, G. Ernest. *Biblical Archaeology.* Philadelphia: The Westminster Press, 1959.

Wright, G. G. Neill. *The Writing of Arabic Numerals.* London: University of London Press, Ltd., 1952.

Wright, William. *Lectures on the Comparative Grammar of the Semitic Languages.* Cambridge: The University Press, 1890.

Articles and Periodicals

Ackroyd, Peter R. "The 153 Fishes in John 21:11 — A Further Note," *The Journal of Theological Studies.* X, April, 1959.

Albright, William F. "An Aramaean Magical Text in Hebrew from the Seventh Century B.C.," *Bulletin of the American Schools of Oriental Research.* No. 76, Dec. 1939.

————. "The Lachish Letters after Five Years," *Bulletin of the American Schools of Oriental Research* No. 82, April 1941.

————. "Reexamination of the Lachish Letters," *Bulletin of the American Schools of Oriental Research.* No. 73, Feb. 1939.

Allis, Oswald T. "The Punishment of the Men of Bethshemesh," *The Evangelical Quarterly,* XV, No. 4, Oct. 1943.

Allrik, H. L. "The Lists of Zerubbabel (Nehemiah 7 and Ezra 2) and the Hebrew Numeral Notation," *Bulletin of the American Schools of Oriental Research.* No. 136, Dec. 1954.

Anderson, W. French. "Arithmetical Procedure in Minoan Linear A and in Minoan-Greek Linear B.," *American Journal of Archaeology.* LXII, No. 3, July 1958.

Ap-Thomas, D. R. "A Numerical Poser," *Journal of Near Eastern Studies.* II, Number 3, July 1943.

Baron, Salo. "The Authenticity of the Numbers in the Historical Books of the Old Testament," *Journal of Biblical Literature.* XLIX, 1930.

Byington, Steven T. "A Mathematical Approach to Hebrew Meters," *Journal of Biblical Literature.* LXVI, Part I, March 1947.

Campbell, Edward F. "The Amarna Letters and the Amarna Period," *The Biblical Archaeologist.* XXIII, Feb. 1960.

Clark, R. E. D. "The Large Numbers of the Old Testament," *Journal of the Transactions of the Victoria Institute.* LXXXVII.

Cook, H. J. "Pekah," *Vetus Testamentum.* XIV, No. 2, April 1964.

Coleman, A. J. "Faith and Math," *Christian Education.* XXXII, June 1949.

Dow, Sterling. "Greek Numerals," *American Journal of Archaeology.* LVI, Jan. 1952.

Dunning, Frederick. "Ku Klux Fulfills the Scripture," *The Christian Century.* XLI, No. 38, Sept. 1924.

Eerdmans, B. D. "The Composition of Numbers," *Oudtestamentische Studien.* VI, 1949.

Emerton, J. A. "The Hundred and Fifty-three Fishes in John 21:11," *The Journal of Theological Studies.* IX, April 1958.

Farrer, A. M. "Loaves and Thousands," *The Journal of Theological Studies.* IV, 1953.

Fraenkel, Abraham A. "Jewish Mathematics and Astronomy," *Scripta Mathematica.* XXV, 1960.

Finkel, Joshua. "A Mathematical Conundrum in the Ugaritic Keret Poem," *Hebrew Union College Annual.* XXVI, 1955.

Gandz, Solomon. "Complementary Fractions in Bible and Talmud," *American Academy for Jewish Research.* Jubilee Volume, 1945.

————. "Hebrew Numerals," *American Academy for Jewish Research.* IV, 1932-33.

Ginsberg, H. L. "Lachish Ostraca New and Old," *Bulletin of the American Schools of Oriental Research.* No. 80, Dec. 1940.

Ginsburg, Jekuthiel. "Rabbi Ben Ezra on Permutations and Combinations," *Mathematics Teacher.* XV, October 1922.

Gordis, Robert. "The Heptad as an Element of Biblical and Rabbinic Style," *Journal of Biblical Literature.* LXII, 1943.

Gordon, Cyrus H. "The Minoan Bridge: Newest Frontier in Biblical Studies," *Christianity Today.* March 15, 1963.

Heath, T. L. "Greek Mathematics and Science," *Mathematics Gazette.* XXXII, July 1948.

Keller, Henry. "Numerics in Old Hebrew Medical Lore," *Scripta Mathematica, I.* XXXII, 1935.

Kennedy, Gerald T. "The Use of Numbers in Sacred Scripture," *American Ecclesiastical Review.* LXXXIX, No. 1, July 1958.

Keyser, C. J. "The Spiritual Significance of Mathematics," *Religious Education.* IV, April 1911—Feb. 1912.

König, Eduard. "Number," *A Dictionary of the Bible.* ed. James Hastings. New York: Charles Scribner's Sons, 1923.

Lucas, A. "The Number of Israel at the Exodus," *Palestine Exploration Quarterly.* 1944.

Maritain, Jacques. "God and Science," *University.* Winter 1962.

McCown, C. C. "The Density of Population in Ancient Israel," *Journal of Biblical Literature.* 1947.

Mendenhall, George E. "The Census Lists of Numbers 1 and 26," *Journal of Biblical Literature.* LXVII, March 1958.

——————. "Covenant Forms in Israelite Tradition," *The Biblical Archaeologist,* XVII, No. 3.

Muirhead, L. A. "Numbers," *Dictionary of the Apostolic Church.* ed. James Hastings. New York: Charles Scribner's Sons, 1918.

Panin, Ivan. "Bible Numerics," *Things to Come.* XVII, XVIII, Feb., March, May-Dec., 1911; Jan., Feb., April, May, July, November, 1912.

Patrides, C. A. "The Numerological Approach to Cosmic Order During the English Renaissance," *Isis.* XLIX, 1958.

Pope, M. H. "Numbers," *The Interpreter's Dictionary of the Bible.* Nashville: Abingdon Press, 1962.

Quievreux, Francois. "La Structure Symbolique de L'Evangile de Saint Jean," *Revue D'Histoire et de Philosophie Religieuses.* Paris: Presses Universitaires de France, 1953.

Rahtjen, B. D. "A Note Concerning the Form of the Gezer Tablet," *Palestine Exploration Quarterly.* Jan.—June, 1961.

Rainey, A. F. "The Kingdom of Ugarit," *The Biblical Archaeologist.* XXVIII, Dec. 1965.

Robbins, Charles J. "A Fish Story," *The Priest.* XIV, Dec. 1960.

Roth, W. M. W. "The Numerical Sequence $x/x+1$ in the Old Testament," *Vetus Testamentum.* XXII, July, 1962.

Sachs, A. J. "Some Metrological Problems in Old Babylonian Mathematical Texts," *Bulletin of the American Schools of Oriental Research.* XCVI, Dec. 1944.

Schippers, Reinier. "Paul and the Computer," *Christianity Today*. Dec. 4, 1964.

Segal, J. B. "Numerals in the Old Testament," *Journal of Semitic Studies*. X, No. 1, Spring 1965.

Seidenberg, A. "The Ritual Origin of Counting," *Archive for History of Exact Sciences, II*. Nov. 16, 1962.

Smith, William T. "Number," *The International Standard Bible Encyclopedia*. IV, ed. James Orr. Chicago: The Howard-Severance Co., 1925.

Von Allmen, J. J. "Numbers," *A Companion to the Bible*. New York: Oxford University Press, 1958.

Yeivin, S. "Was there a High Portal in the First Temple?" *Vetus Testamentum*. XIV, No. 3, July 1964.

Unpublished Material

Rea, John. "The Historical Setting of the Exodus and Conquest." Winona Lake: Grace Theological Seminary, 1958 (Th.D. Dissertation).

INDEX

Subject Index

Abraham 50
Acrophonic Numerals . . 29
Addition 50
Ahab 52
Akkadian 97
  Literature 154
Antediluvian Ages . . . 56
Amarna
  Letters 117
  Period 63
Apocrypha 109
Aramaeans 45
Aramaic 31-32
  Documents . . . . 137ff.
  Numbers 31-33
  Texts 100
  Versions 20
Assyrian laws 102

Baal 98, 100
Babylonia 29-30
  Scribes of 106
Beth-shemesh . . . 55, 87-88

Canaan
  Conquest of . . . . 65ff.
  Population of . . . . 63ff.
Cardinal Numbers 26-27, 40-41
Census Lists . . .58, 75, 79ff.
Chariots . . . . . . 84f.
Climactic Use of Numbers 93ff.
Coins 38-39

David 55, 79, 83, 99
Dead Sea Scrolls . 19, 38, 90
Deborah 61

Edomites 62

Egypt 26, 29, 51, 66
  Documents from . . . 107
  Numbers 29, 31
  Scribes of 106
  Texts from 31
Exodus
  Size of . . . . . . 58ff.

Firstborn 78
Fractions 50-51

Gematria . . . . . 126ff.
Gezer Calendar . . . 19, 37
Gilgamesh Epic 102
Gnostics . . 112ff., 128, 141
Greece 26, 108
Greek . . . . 40ff.
  Alphabet 140-141
  Notation Systems . . 41-45
Greeks 130

Hebrew 36
  Alphabet 38, 141
  Inscriptions 19
  Manuscripts 20
  Text 26
Hittites 102

Israel 26

Joseph 31
Joshua 66, 85

Keret 50, 97

Lachish Letters 37
Large Numbers . . . . 55ff.
Levi, Tribe of 77

Manna 60

Mari Texts 85
Martin Luther 145
Masoretic Text . . . 33, 38
Mathematical Processes . . 49
Mernepta Stela 75
Minoan 35-36
Moabite 37
  Stone 37, 52
Moses 31, 54, 62
Mystical Numbers . . 125ff.

Nabatean 33
Nero 144
Numbers
  Definition of 18
  Notation Systems . . . 28
Numerals 18
  Hebrew 28
Numerology, Definition of . 18

Omri 52
Ordinal Numbers . . 27, 41

Philistines 64, 83-84
Phoenicia . . 31, 35, 40, 64
Pseudepigrapha 109
Pyramidology 155
Pythagoras . . 107-109, 126

Qumran 45
  Literature of 109

Ramses II 66
Red Sea 59
Rome 26
Rounded Numbers . . . 51

Samaria 34
Saul 53, 87, 99
Shalmanezer III 85
Shishak 85
Siloam Inscription . . . 36
Sinai, Climate of . . . 60f.
Sumerian 106-107
  King List 57
  Numbers 29-30
Symbolic Numbers . . 103ff.

Tell ed-Duweir 34
Textual Problems
  Omissions 86-87
  Transmission . . . 87-90

Ugaritic
  Literature . 50, 95-98, 100,
  117ff., 154
  Numbers . 30-31, 33, 37, 45
United Monarchy 16

Scripture Index

GENESIS
1:1 139
2:3 116
2:4 74
4:15 118
Genesis 5 . . . . 56, 57, 58
5:3-31 51
13:16 26
15:5 25
15:41 25
15:49 25

18:2 143
18:28 50
20:16 54
20:35 54
26:12 54
29:20 118
29:27 118
34:30 25
36:15 70
41:49 25
41:53 118

47:24 51
49:10 143

EXODUS

1:2 78
1:5 90
1:8 69
2:16 118
6:16 78
7:7 54
12:37 . . . . . 58, 59
14:7 84
15:22-26 60
Exodus 16 60
16:13 60
16:36 51
17:5-7 60
18:13 62
18:13-17 62
18:14 62
18:18 62
18:21 75
18:21f. 62
20:15 84
21:2 118
25:10 51
25:17 51
30:12 26
30:13 26
30:14 26
32:28 54
38:21 78

LEVITICUS

15:13 25
23:13 51
25:8 . . . . . . 25, 50
26:18 54

NUMBERS

Numbers 1. 55, 56, 58, 59, 67,
   68, 70, 71, 72, 73

1:3 26
1:19 26
1:20-46 50
1:23 70
1:25 . . . . . . 70, 75
1:46 . . . . 69, 73, 75
1:49 26
2:32 . . . . 69, 73, 75
3:4 77
3:39 77
3:47ff. 50
4:48 77
9:20 25
11:31 60
11:32 60
11:34 79
14:8 94
14:29 79
14:32 79
14:35 79
20:1 79
20:7-12 60
20:14-21 62
20:20 62
20:21 62
23:1 118
23:10 26
23:14 118
23:29 118
Numbers 25 76
25:9 76
25:14 76
Numbers 26 . 55, 56, 58, 59,
   67, 68, 71, 73
26:9 76
26:10 76
26:11 77
26:51 . . . . 69, 73, 75
26:62 77
28:11 118
28:19 118
28:27 118

31:27ff. 50
31:32-40 69

DEUTERONOMY
1:11 54
2:46 63
2:5 63
2:14 79
2:15 79
4:15 49
5:9 94
7:9 54
10:6 79
16:9 25
17:6 . . . . . 94, 101
28:7 118
28:25 118
30:12 143
32:30 . . . . . 93, 94
34:6 79
34:7 54

JOSHUA
Joshua 1 71
Joshua 8 85
15:24 83

JUDGES
3:11 54
3:31 83
4:13 84
Judges 5 61
5:4 61
5:30 . . . . . 93, 101
5:31 54
6:15 73
7:3 71
7:4 71
7:6 . . . . . . 25, 71
7:15 25
8:28 54
13:10 54

14:12 118
15:15 83
20:15 85

I SAMUEL
2:11 94
6:19 . . . . 55, 69, 87
9:8 51
10:19 73
11:8 . . . . . . 26, 84
13:1 86
13:5 . . . . . . 55, 84
13:15 26
15:2 83
15:4 83
15:9 83
15:20 83
15:24 83
16:10 118
18:7 . . . . . . 94, 99
29:5 94

II SAMUEL
8:2 82
10:6 85
17:1 85
18:2 51
21:6 118
II Samuel 24 . . . 80, 81
24:2-12 81
24:3 54
24:9 . . . . . . 55, 79
24:10 25
24:13 89

I KINGS
2:11 54
3:8 26
7:23 50
16:23 52
16:29 52
20:30 69

II KINGS

6:10 93
9:32 . . . . . 94, 101
12:11 26
13:9 94
19:35 84

I CHRONICLES

14:9 55
15:11 55
I Chronicles 21 80
21:5 . . . . . . 55, 80
21:12 89
22:14 55
23:3 77
27:1-15 83
27:4 . . . . . . 80, 81

II CHRONICLES

12:3 85
14:8 84

EZRA

Ezra 2 33
6:17 26
10:13 . . . . . . 93, 101

NEHEMIAH

5:11 51
Nehemiah 7 53
13:20 93

JOB

5:19 . . . . . . 94, 119
14:16 25
15:5 70
31:41 25
33:14 . . . . . . 93, 94
33:29 94
33:33 70
35:11 70

38:37 25
40:5 95

PSALMS

12:6 119
56:9 25
62:11 93
68:7-9 60
91:7 . . . . . . 94, 98
105:40 60
119:164 119
147:4 . . . . . . 25, 26

PROVERBS

6:16 94
22:25 70
30:15 94
30:18 . . . . . . 94, 99
30:21 94
30:29 94

ECCLESIASTES

8:12 54

ISAIAH

17:6 . . . . . . 94, 101
53:12 26
65:12 26

JEREMIAH

11:19 70
36:23 94

EZEKIEL

46:14 51

HOSEA

6:2 84
12:16 25

AMOS

1:3 94
1:6 94

1:9 94
1:11 95
1:13 94
2:1 94
2:4 94
2:6 94
4:8 84

MICAH
5:2 73
5:4 94
5:5 95

MATTHEW
10:30 40
18:20 101
19:29 54

LUKE
12:7 40
14:38 40
22:3 40

JOHN
2:6 101
6:10 40
21:11 . . . . . 111, 147

ACTS
6:7 40
7:14 90
7:23 54

11:21 40
13:18 53
13:20 52

I CORINTHIANS
10:5 79

COLOSSIANS
1:2 111
4:13 111
4:15-16 111

II THESSALONIANS
2:7 147
2:8 147

II TIMOTHY
3:16 20

JUDE
Jude 5 79

REVELATION
1:4 111
1:12 111
1:16 111
1:20 111
5:1 111
7:9 40
13:18 . . 40, 103, 111, 147
20:8 40